An INGLORIOUS AFFAIR

An INGLORIOUS AFFAIR

A Decade of Dissent among Suffolk Nonconformists

DAVID HOLMES

The Salters Lane Press

Published by The Salters Lane Press
5 Salters Lane Walpole Halesworth Suffolk IP19 9BA

~

~

ISBN 0-9542259-0-2

~

Designed and typeset in *Minion* and *Gill Sans* by Linda Holmes
The Salters Lane Press Walpole Halesworth Suffolk IP19 9BA

Printed and bound by The Five Castles Press
Raeburn Road South Ipswich Suffolk IP3 0ET

PREFACE

For the past fifteen years we have lived in Walpole, a village near Halesworth in north-east Suffolk. Our garden shares a boundary with the chapel ground of the seventeenth century Independent Meeting House, now known as Walpole Old Chapel – 'Old' because in the 1860s it needed to be distinguished from the village's new Primitive Methodist chapel. Hanging on a wall of this remarkable building the visitor finds two framed posters of 1871. One advertises a harvest tea meeting at which a new pastor is to be ordained. The other mysteriously announces the 'unavoidable postponement' of that event due to 'adverse circumstances which will be fully explained'.

I could find no convincing explanation of these adverse circumstances until, some years later, I came across a substantial bundle of correspondence in the Suffolk Record Office at Ipswich relating to a serious squabble which had taken place in the Independent Church at Halesworth around 1870 and which, incidentally, shed much light on that 1871 row about a new pastor at Walpole. The letters flew with some momentum between the main combatants. It was an absorbing discovery, but more pressing things prevented me from going deeper into the affair. Now, with permission from the Suffolk Congregational Union, I have put most of them (some are carbon copies, others merely notes for letters) at the core of this book. In some cases I have used an extract only, others are printed in their entirety because I thought their style and mood warranted that.

These letters, however, tell only part of the story. They belong to the tempestuous centre of what was a ten-year schism within Halesworth's Congregational community. The church's own documents are equally important in forming a balanced view, over a longer period, of what their own historian, James Newby called, in the discreet 1930s, 'A Dark Period' in the church's history.

A nonconformist church is a far more rewarding entity to study than its Anglican equivalent. That is because a Congregational Church, like its Baptist neighbour, was governed by its members together with its minister; and its ups and downs were recorded, to some extent at least, in its Church Book and the minute book of its deacons. Most of the Halesworth material is preserved in the Lowestoft branch of the Suffolk Record Office, deposited there by a former minister, the late Rev. Ben Angell, and the Church Secretary of his time, Gilbert Burroughes. I am grateful to the present Minister and Elders of what is now Halesworth

United Reformed Church for permitting me to quote extensively from those documents. Mrs Pat Potts, the present Church Secretary, has smoothed paths and unlocked doors in the friendliest of ways. I was also allowed to compile the names of those who, as far as I could disentangle them, were Members of the church at the time of these events. That, possibly incomplete, list is printed as an Appendix. A piece of the puzzle which is still missing is the Church Book, or any written records, of Joseph Harvey's breakaway congregation, meeting in the Halesworth Assembly Room during the ten years of these troubles. I have hunted high and low for them, but without success.

I hope readers will not find it too difficult to navigate the waters of this book. I have deliberately not provided an index, but I hope the dating on each page, the dated contents list, and the *Who Was Who?* at the end will keep everyone on course. I have also risked compiling a list of definitions. I say 'risked' because some controversy still continues about what some of these terms mean.

Any outsider coming new to nonconformist history needs advice and assistance. I have needed a lot of it. I express my special thanks to Professor Clyde Binfield, editor of the *Journal of the United Reformed Church History Society*, for his stimulating interest in my project and for allowing me to read his doctoral thesis of 1965, *Nonconformity in the Eastern Counties 1840-1885, with Reference to its Social Background*. He also commented most helpfully on my text. My thanks also go to Peter Northeast, Gilbert Burroughes, the Rev. Kenneth Maltus Smith, Sheila and Michael Gooch, Rachel Lawrence, Pat Coady, the Haward family and many others in Halesworth and elsewhere for their help and advice. I say with more than usual conviction: 'any errors which remain are mine and mine alone'.

I have been much helped by staff at both the Lowestoft and Ipswich branches of the Suffolk Record Office; the Norfolk Record Office; the Norfolk Studies Library; the Essex Record Office; the Newham Local Studies Library; The Woolwich Local Studies Library; the British Library; Dr Williams's Library, and the House of Lords Record Office. Mike Fordham, Curator of the Halesworth and District Museum, and Janet Huckle have searched out some gems from the museum's photographic collection. The Minister and Secretary of the Union Church, Hunstanton, have allowed me to show their photograph of R.A. Cliff. Finally, I have to offer more than thanks to my wife Linda for designing the book, seeing it through to publication and being an exacting critic.

Throughout my assembly of this chronicle there has been an imp at my shoulder asking why I should think I was competent to deal with this piece of local religious history. Apart from quoting my old experience in political journalism and the attendant teasing out of facts, I found him difficult to answer. On the one hand, I can say I am thoroughly nonconformist by blood: my mother's family traces its line back to no less a Calvinist than John Knox; and parts of my father's family were Plymouth Brethren. Yet I grew up an Anglican, much attracted by sung evensong at any cathedral within reach; and as a young wartime soldier trailing along the Yorkshire Ouse to Bishopthorpe on Sunday afternoons, in the company of Archbishop Lang's great-nephew, to have tea with, or at least sit at the table of, Archbishop Garbett. Those green fields of religious influence have since been subject to repeated 'set-aside' and have now become rather stony ground.

I thought I should come clean about all this so that it might be clear (in today's horrid phrase) where I was 'coming from', or rather where not. All I can promise is that I have unearthed all the relevant facts I could find and presented them as fairly as I know how.

David Holmes
Walpole, 2002

SOME DEFINITIONS

DISSENTERS – A general term with both religious and political connotations. Dissenters were protestants who, in the main, rejected the teaching and organisation of the Established Church of England. By the nineteenth century many had come to accept the doctrinal aspects of the Thirty-nine Articles, but few could agree with the concept of an Established Church whatever its organisation. For nearly 200 years they had suffered politically and socially for their beliefs, but by the middle of that century dissenting town councillors, JPs and MPs were becoming increasingly common.

NONCONFORMISTS – A term roughly synonymous with the above, but more in use after the middle of the nineteenth century. With the gradual recovery of their political rights, they gained growing national influence. The term covers Congregationalists and English Presbyterians (since 1972 joined in the United Reformed Church), Baptists, Methodists, and Quakers.

INDEPENDENTS – A seventeenth century term for those Congregational dissenters who were not content to reform existing Anglican congregations, but established separate churches, free of any external control or influence. By the mid-nineteenth century the term, though still in use as at Halesworth, was regarded as decidedly old fashioned. It would then have been synonymous with 'congregational' – hence the breakaway church became known as the 'New Congregational Church'.

MINISTERS/PASTORS – Congregational ministers, while having substantial influence, had no authority over a church. Working in concert with the deacons (see below), they were answerable to the Church Meeting, at which all accredited members of the church were entitled to speak and vote. This balance of power has often encouraged notable partnerships between pastors and people, but it has also caused stresses and even open hostility. A distinguished nineteenth century Congregationalist (Rev. J. A. James of Carrs Lane, Birmingham) wrote that 'in many of our churches the pastor is depressed far below his just level. He has no official distinction or authority. He may flatter like a sycophant, he may beg like a servant, he may woo like a lover, but he is not permitted to enjoin like a ruler. His opinion is treated with no deference, his person treated with no respect...he is only permitted to peep and mutter from the dust'. This particular minister, however, was venerated by his congregation.

ORDINATION – This, for Congregationalists and Baptists, was the event at which a person's calling to the Ministry was recognised and sanctioned by prayer and by the laying on of hands: the hands being those of fellow ministers and lay officers of the church. If he later moved to be the pastor of another church he would be 'recognised' or 'inducted'; although, in the nineteenth century, the term 'ordained' was often used to describe this event also.

DEACONS – Lay Members of a Congregational (or Baptist) church, sufficiently respected to be entrusted with its government. Elected by the Church Meeting, a deacon might hold the post for life or for some other fixed term. Congregational deacons became 'elders' after their union with the Presbyterians in 1972 to form the United Reformed Church.

CHAPEL/CHURCH – In the context of this book, a 'chapel' is a building in which nonconformists meet. A 'church' is the body of people who are 'the gathered fellowship of believers', and constitute the core of a congregation.

INTRODUCTION

HALESWORTH – THE TOWN AND ITS PEOPLE

What follows has the makings of a drama; a drama set on a small stage, involving only a handful of people in an isolated corner of East Anglia. But whatever the scale, the intensity of differing human beliefs, the interaction of all too human personalities, always sets a stage alight. The intention of these opening pages is to describe briefly the background against which the action is to be played out.

The action in question took place between 1866 and 1877 among the Congregationalists of Quay Street Independent Church in the small market town of Halesworth in north-east Suffolk. At that time the population of the town, and the handful of farming villages scattered round it, was no more than three to four thousand. The Independents, perhaps two hundred in number, were neither the poor nor the wealthy, but they made up a substantial proportion of the solid middle class of traders and shopkeepers and farmers of the Halesworth district. They were, in a real sense, the core of the place. And many of them still bore the Puritan fervour and astringency which marked this area in the critical days of the Civil War and after.

Flowing through Halesworth, now as then, is a river which eventually becomes the Blyth – little more than a big stream as it enters from the west, but at this time made navigable for the ten miles to the east, past the old quay at Blythburgh and down the wide estuary to the open sea at Southwold. This navigable stretch, with its six locks, was the achievement of the Blyth Navigation, founded as a thriving trading link a hundred years before but now in decline. For that century, the merchants of Halesworth, proud of their tiny inland Quay, and those of Southwold, with their restored harbour, had competed keenly and profitably. Shallow-draught wherries had brought coal and timber up the river to Halesworth and carried malt and grain back on to seagoing craft. Such trade must have brought a familiar whiff of the ocean to this inland community, some of whose farmworkers spent each winter at sea with the fishing boats of Lowestoft and Yarmouth.

Every market town has close links with its farming hinterland. In Halesworth that relationship was even more intimate, with several farmhouses being part of the town, their farm buildings and land immediately behind. The area had been well-known for its dairy farming, but the gently rolling landscape of the Blyth Valley had by this time turned to cereals, much of it high quality malting barley. Its large

Halesworth & District Museum

Quay Street. The Halesworth Independent chapel stands back, half way along on the right, the maltings complex opposite. This is about the turn of the century – paved pedestrian ways, but still a dirt road.

complex of maltings and breweries – among East Anglia's best – dominated the townscape, the largest of them facing the Independent Chapel. Round the gently raised rim, stood perhaps six windmills belonging to the town's milling families.

Although the clouds of depression were gathering, the local economy was healthy. The Congregational family of Aldred no longer made fine hempen linen at their factory in Chediston Street, but they were successful shopkeepers in Market Place, selling woollens and silks and carpets; and fine old Cheshire cheese at 5d a lb. The *Halesworth Times* advertised their 'usual Christmas shilling parcel' of Emperor tea, raisins, currants, good sugar, peel and chestnuts. Samuel Smith's firm in Bridge Street made smart carriages for the London trade and had taken out a patent on a special door-opening device. Banks had been established, some to flourish, some to fail. Halesworth's iron and brass foundry was doing good business making agricultural machinery. John Gostling, the Market Place pharmeceutical chemist, was a worshipper at Quay Street. Among the items of bodily care offered to his customers was 'Essence of Horseradish, an eightpenny bottle of which might be relied upon as one of the best applications for rheumatism, gout and numbness of the limbs etc'.

Close by the Congregational Chapel in Quay Street was the grocer's shop of Samuel Brown, for decades a deacon of the chapel, a Baptist from Bury St Edmunds turned strict Independent. Alongside it, the King's Head coaching inn was run by Nathan Chipperfield, later to be a Congregational deacon. Also in Quay Street were the premises of John Day, printer, bookseller and china dealer, and Superintendent of the Chapel's Sunday School.

Further out on the road to Holton was Castle House where Joseph Benjamin Harvey, and his father before him, ran an Academy noted for its 'careful attention to the moral and general deportment of the pupils'. Harvey was not only a deacon of the Quay Street chapel but its organist as well. That position and his own assertive character were to bring him rapidly into the centre of this tale.

Of other prominent Church members we shall hear rather less: Walter Ives, with a boot factory in Bridge Street; Alfred Smith, local Inland Revenue officer; William Wigg, clockmaker of Thoroughfare; Henry Cornish, shoemaker in Pound Street; William Took, baker and confectioner in Thoroughfare; Elizabeth Mannall, milliner and dressmaker in Market Place; William Rignall, gunsmith, also in Market Place. However, John Bedwell, tax collector of Bungay Road, a man of ultra-strict temperament, formerly a Baptist, will have a key part to play towards the end. Leaders or followers, they were part of the backbone of this church and of the community they lived in. The memorial stones of many of them stand in the unconsecrated, nonconformist, sector of Halesworth cemetery which by Act of Parliament took over from the bulging parish graveyard in 1855. Paupers and dissenters were excluded from the main part of the cemetery – those greener acres blessed by the bishop of the Established Church.

Central to the whole proceedings will be three brothers of the Haward family, a name of great importance at that time and still significant in Halesworth today. All three were neighbouring farmers a few miles away in the Bramfield area. Robert Haward (to whom *Kelly's Directory* gave the title of Esq.) at Mells Hill, George Haward at Manor Farm and Charles Haward at Holly Farm. The very different roles they played will be described as the story moves on. Two of them lie buried beside the Bramfield village chapel, built on their father's land in 1841.

For a remote but significant country town Halesworth was an up-to-date little place. The railway had linked it to Norwich and Yarmouth in 1854, to Ipswich and London five years later. The stage coach had long since ceased to call at the Angel Inn: there were faster and more comfortable ways to travel. The Halesworth gas works had opened in 1838. A year or two later, the running cost of the town's 41 gas lamps had been one shilling and ninepence (about nine new pence) for every hour 'during the dark nights of the moon'. The Independent Chapel lay only a small pipe-run from the gas works. It had some handsome gaslights of its own.

The health and sanitary conditions of the place were quite shaming. In 1871 a Home Office inspector severely criticised the Halesworth Vestry (forerunner of the local council) for its incompetent dealing with the town's sewage. A committee of townspeople – half of them Congregationalists – were ordered to put things right. Yet sanitation was to remain seriously inadequate for years to come. Privies, whether inside or out, usually drained into open cesspools, only slightly less objectionable than the midden heaps which the night-cart carried out of sight down a track dubbed Honeypot Lane. In 1871 there were perhaps a dozen water closets, flushed by bucket, but they all drained straight into the town river, where there was insufficient flow to keep things moving. Water supplies were poor and often impure. Many private houses had their own wells. The town pumps, in Market Place and elsewhere, poured forth apparently pure water, nobody dreaming that wells or underground streams could themselves be contaminated. Village people who had no well still carried the water from local ponds: 'pond fever' would be common in Suffolk for decades to come. The water-borne diseases of cholera and typhoid broke out at times, very few understanding why. In the 1850s Thompson George, the Halesworth maltster and brewer, had called for main sewerage, but in vain. He was doubtless prompted by the needs of his own business; but perhaps also by the obsessive reformer Edwin Chadwick who campaigned, with only limited success, to banish filth, overcrowding, disease, crime and inefficient government from Britain. Main drainage would not come to the town until the 1950s.

Smallpox, at least, was being treated seriously. Jenner's vaccination technique had been made compulsory by statute in 1853. But a few years later a government inspector reported that 20 per-cent of the 954 schoolchildren examined in the local Blything Hundred workhouse refused vaccination, so strong was parental prejudice. Nevertheless, Dr Pryce Morris, public vaccinator and private practitioner, was looking after his smallpox patients at the Pest House high up on Loampits Lane.

Like most small towns of the time, Halesworth's streets were unpaved, though with stone walkways to keep feet out of the mud. Dry when the weather was dry, the streets were soon churned up by horsedrawn traffic after rain. The network of eighteenth century turnpike roads remained, but often in disrepair. Each Suffolk parish still bore the cost of maintaining these roads, one of which passed through Halesworth on its way from the south to Beccles and Bungay. Few parishes looked after their roads efficiently. Those who did took their materials from the workhouse, where male paupers were required by government order to break seven hundredweight of stone a day. The poor who could stand the draconian regime of the Bulcamp workhouse – 244 of them in 1871 – found at least relative security there. But husbands were permanently separated from their wives, and children from their parents. Despite the work of reformers, society still regarded poverty as a state brought on themselves by inadequate individuals – or as some dissenters put it, 'poverty is the consequence of sin'. The courts took a similar view. Inmates of the poorhouse who kicked over the traces (described as 'refractory paupers') could receive severe punishment. In 1877, two men slipped out of Bulcamp, got a bit drunk in the White Hart at Blythburgh and broke some windows on their return. The Yoxford bench declared them 'rogues and vagabonds' and sentenced them to a month's hard labour in Ipswich Gaol. The magistrates who put them there were high Anglican landlords. But it cannot be assumed that the self-made farmers and traders who were Halesworth's Independents, while largely Liberal politically, were at all liberal when it came to social policy. Their forebears had not been in favour of improving the Poor Law and they certainly did not like the rising trades unions – especially Joseph Arch's efforts in the 1870s to improve the lot of agricultural workers. Even worshipping farmers were not averse to putting their poverty-stricken workers on out-door relief so that the parish rather than the employer paid their wages. It should be recorded, however, that in 1873 the Quay Street church petitioned Parliament in support of Plimsoll's Bill to make seamen's lives safer.

The law in general was administered by Halesworth's police force,

Superintendant Jeremiah Gobbett (a local dissenting name) and two constables. Their preoccupation was with the drunkenness unavoidable in a town with as many pubs and beer houses as this. When a policeman was murdered in Halesworth in 1862 the culprit was publicly hanged, with 4000 people watching, on top of the County Hall in Ipswich – the last public execution in Suffolk before parliament forebade the practice.

Halesworth had better schools than average even before the Liberals' 1870 Act laid the basis for compulsory free schooling. Suffolk as a whole was to achieve an astonishing literacy rate of more than 90% by the end of the century. One obstacle had been the reluctance of many farmers to free local children from working as cheap labour on the land. The price of the corn, rather than the state of their education, marked the well-being of the society which had bred them.

CHURCH AND CHAPEL

For centuries St Mary's Church had been the only religious building in Halesworth, standing on a slight prominence within the town. The fourteenth century tower still sounded with a peal of fifteenth century bells. The traces of an earlier round tower, and some Saxon stonework here and there, showed its origins might lie well before the Norman conquest. Until the last years of the eighteenth century, its clergy had been the undisputed guardians of the souls of Halesworth – sixteen hundred and seventy six of them in the census of 1801.

By no means all of them welcomed the Anglican Church's pastoral care. Dissenters put it more strongly. 'This town was suffered to be in a state of awful darkness until a little light began to break in upon some of the people, which gradually increased like the dawn of day', says the Church Book of Halesworth's group of Independents who gathered in 1793 at the house of Hustings Moore in Pound Street.

That was late for a Suffolk town to gain its first dissenting congregation; but that was not due to any reluctance to embrace the old Puritanism. For 150 years Halesworth people had walked or ridden out to the Independent Meeting House at Walpole, one of the first Puritan congregations set up after the Civil War and occupying a sixteenth century timber-framed farmhouse converted, over some decades, into a chapel.

For these Walpole Independents, a mile or two out of Halesworth, reforming the English Church from within, a process which had continued ever since Henry VIII's break with Rome, was not radical enough. They believed there had to be a new start and in 1649 they were among the first to make it, rejecting such institutions as bishops, the *Book of Common Prayer*, surplices, kneeling, bowing of the head. With Calvinist

Halesworth & District Museum

Turn-of-the-century Halesworth from the tower of the parish church. Market Place lies in the left foreground. The tall chimney in the middle distance belongs to the old iron foundry. The Quay Street Chapel stands close to the distant trees on the left.

fervour, they believed themselves to be predestined 'saints', who would obey neither bishops nor presbyters but govern themselves. The congregation had grown steadily, gathered from miles around.

But at the end of the eighteenth century, Walpole's congregation does not seem to have been the exciting and radical entity it once was. The countryside was beginning to suffer from depopulation. What may have been more influential was that the Walpole minister of the time, John Walker, was nearly 80 and perhaps his preaching could not draw the big congregations of the past. The newly-gathered dissenters of Pound Street, Halesworth, however, had found a remarkable pastor in John Dennant and grew to the point, in 1836, where a much larger place was needed. This was built in Quay Street, designed by the innovative chapel architect James Fenton of Chelmsford.

In 1851 a remarkable and unique national census took place. It set out to measure the religious attendances of the country – how many people went to which church or chapel on a particular Sunday in March. The results, although there are many qualifications about their absolute accuracy, shocked the Church of England. The returns showed congregations of 569–854–417 at the three services in Halesworth parish church; while the Independents in Quay Street returned 428–560–205, all these totals were inclusive of Sunday School children. Figures for the town's Wesleyan Methodists (never strong in Suffolk) and Particular Baptists were very much smaller. The Baptists had a small church in Chediston Street, later moving to Loampits Lane.

For the main nonconformist congregation to have achieved something near parity with the Established Church was an important development – and one seen in many parts of the country. It had a political as well as a religious significance. Nonconformists were still fighting to free themselves from some of the penalties imposed on them by the Clarendon Code in the wake of the Civil War and Cromwell's Commonwealth. Their main political rights had been reluctantly restored. But only in 1854 were dissenters given ground in which to bury their own dead; not until 1868 were they excused from paying church rates to maintain the Church of England.

There were dissenters who doggedly carried on these struggles for their full rights. But a few decided that the quickest way to gain a full place in society was by moderating their religious views and joining or rejoining the more socially acceptable Church of England. Success in business or trade made a puritan life style somehow seem less appropriate. There was a social cachet in being seen on the Rectory lawn. Against that, it was the trader and artisan and farmer who had made Dissent the force it had become and was, for some time yet, to remain.

The Church of England was itself changing. It had at first responded

Halesworth & District Museum

The seat of the drama. The Independent Chapel in Halesworth, proud behind its gas lamps and railings. This photograph was probably taken about two decades after the 'Affair'. The awning marks the shop of Deacon Samuel Brown, the grocer. Turn left at the end for the railway station.

far too slowly to the industrial revolution and the subsequent shifts in population. But a revival was taking place. Stirred up by the growth of Methodism, 2000 new Anglican churches had been built in England and Wales. Partly in response, the main nonconformist denominations built over 4000 chapels between 1851 and 1876. Halesworth Independents themselves had already prompted the founding of two chapels in neighbouring villages – Bramfield and Wissett. Others were built by Wesleyans, Primitive Methodists and Baptists. Most of them were in respectable Gothic, leaving Walpole's rustic style looking a bit tatty by comparison.

As the architecture of Congregationalism changed so did the religious atmosphere. New challenges, new dangers appeared. In 1859 Darwin's *Origin of Species* called in question the Bible's account of the Creation. The stately and beautiful language of the Anglican *Book of Common Prayer* began to return, though usually unacknowledged. To sing the words of the psalms was no longer unacceptable.

With the Methodists John and Charles Wesley, and into the nineteenth century, came evangelism and a more robust, even romantic, school of popular religious music. The whole atmosphere was changing. Together with a more fervent style of preaching, the change did much to reinvigorate nonconformity.

By the 1860s 'chants' were being sung in some Congregational churches. These were passages taken from the Prayer Book such as the *Te Deum*, the *Psalms*, and a variety of other scriptural passages. Such changes caused acute discomfort among conservative congregations. A.G. Matthews, distinguished historian of the dissenters, wrote 'The older of us can remember the suspicion incurred, the ostentatious firmness with which some irreconcilables kept their seats while the chant proceeded'.

In 1864, two years before Quay Street's troubles began, the Rev. Henry Allon of the Union Chapel, Islington, declared in his Chairman's address to the English Congregational Union that 'the dogma of verbal inspiration has, in thousands of religious men, produced a widespread revolt'. Belief in an unerring Bible, he said, was an indefensible doctrine. In 1874 a Congregational preacher in King's Lynn said, 'We have left the Puritan era. We no longer despise the beautiful and artistic, but claim them as divine things and enlist them in the divine service. We no longer consider retirement from the world a sign of holiness but believe that all man's life and work can be dedicated to heaven'. A delegate to the 1870 Congregational Union meeting could joke, 'it is in fact extremely doubtful whether there is a devil to be met with anywhere. If he exists now he is an amiable and polite personage, against whom it were bigotry to say anything'.

These were becoming widely held views; that is widely held in pulpits whose celebrated occupants had their sermons reported in the religious press. But it is doubtful if such statements would have had much of a welcome within the Halesworth Independent Church. As with any tendency, there were those who were determined to stand firm against it. And as with any conflict of principle, the personalities of those fighting the battle themselves became part of the issue. That must have been the case in and around Quay Street, Halesworth, during the decade of the story which now unfolds.

Halesworth & District Museum

The Anglican establishment of the town gather on the Rector's spacious lawns. Nonconformists might rejoice in their nearness to God. But some regretted that society's approval could not be theirs as well.

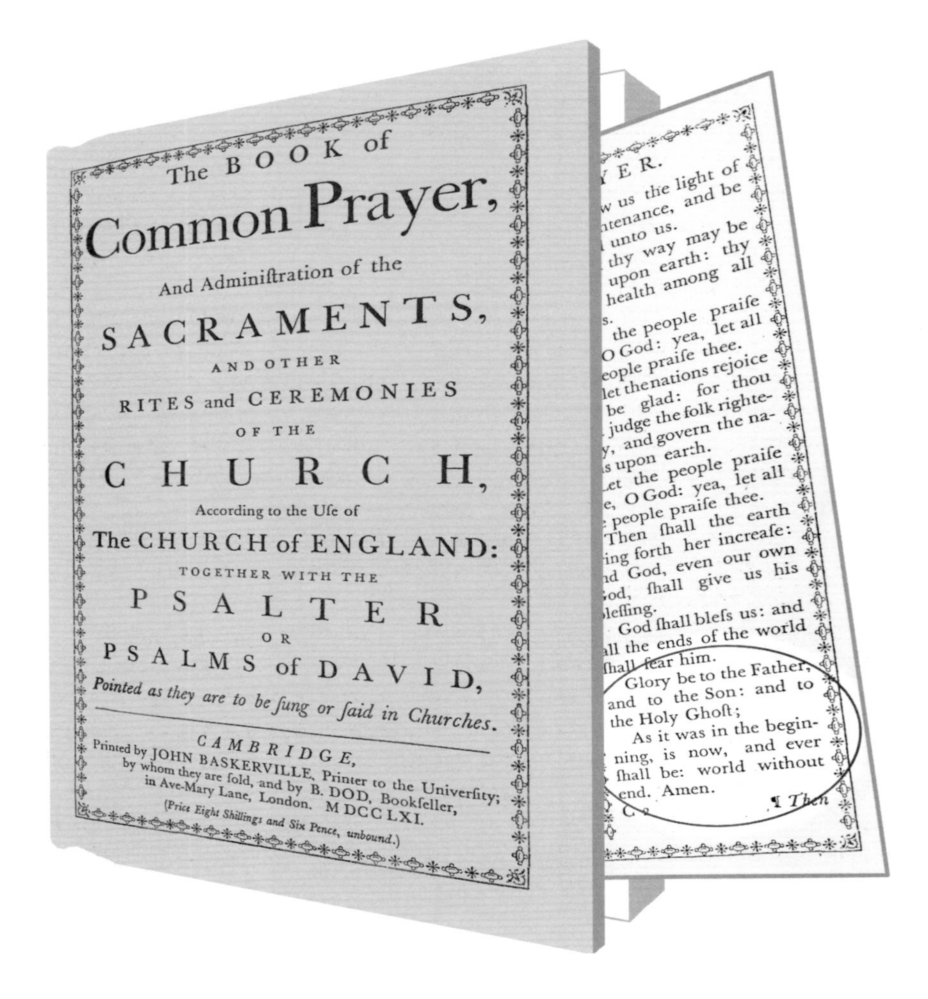

The BOOK of
Common Prayer,
And Adminiſtration of the
SACRAMENTS,
AND OTHER
RITES and CEREMONIES
OF THE
CHURCH,
According to the Uſe of
The CHURCH of ENGLAND:
TOGETHER WITH THE
PSALTER
OR
PSALMS of DAVID,
Pointed as they are to be ſung or ſaid in Churches.

CAMBRIDGE,
Printed by JOHN BASKERVILLE, Printer to the Univerſity;
by whom they are fold, and by B. DOD, Bookſeller,
in Ave-Mary Lane, London. MDCCLXI.
(*Price Eight Shillings and Six Pence, unbound.*)

YER.
w us the light of
ntenance, and be
unto us.
thy way may be
upon earth: thy
health among all
s.
the people praiſe
O God: yea, let all
eople praiſe thee.
let the nations rejoice
be glad: for thou
judge the folk righte-
y, and govern the na-
s upon earth.
et the people praiſe
e, O God: yea, let all
people praiſe thee.
Then ſhall the earth
ing forth her increaſe:
nd God, even our own
od, ſhall give us his
leſſing.
God ſhall bleſs us: and
ll the ends of the world
ſhall fear him.
Glory be to the Father,
and to the Son: and to
the Holy Ghoſt;
As it was in the begin-
ning, is now, and ever
ſhall be: world without
end. Amen.
¶ Then

Illustration based on an edition of 1761 in the library of the University of East Anglia, Norwich

1
RUPTURE
1866–1868

The familiar words circled opposite, to be found in the *Book of Common Prayer*, are known as the shorter *Gloria*. They date back perhaps to 400 AD and are one of Christianity's oldest expressions of religious praise. Churches of every sort have said or sung them for over a 1000 years.

But the sixteenth century protestant reformer John Calvin of Geneva forebade the use of the *Gloria* because its precise words did not appear in the Bible. English Puritans, strongly influenced by Calvin's teachings, followed his example. In the wake of the Civil War, Parliament had banned such sentences by statute. This is the story of what happened to one nineteenth century nonconformist congregation – the Independents of Quay Street, Halesworth – when its organist and choirmaster tried to incorporate the *Gloria* into its services.

The organist, Joseph Benjamin Harvey,[1] believed in relaxing the severity of the church's services, including a more generous use of music. In 1859, when organs were still rare in chapels, he had persuaded these Independents to buy their first instrument.[2] Previously the singing had been led by the Halesworth draper, William Aldred, with the aid of a tuning fork or pitch-pipe.[3]

The puritanism of early Independents and Congregationalists had begun slowly to soften. If the *Book of Common Prayer* was too much associated with the Church of England to be acceptable in non-conformist circles, it contained some of the most beautiful prayers in the English language, and these had crept in to Congregational use despite the strong preference for spontaneous prayer. This same apprehension applied to the *Gloria* itself. It was feared by some as the first step in re-establishing a Liturgy, that is a prescribed form of worship, within a church which had for two hundred years firmly rejected such things – the very cause of their dissent.

1 J.B. Harvey (1825-1891), head of Castle Academy for Boys from 1855, deacon of Quay Street church, organist and choirmaster.

2 Supplied by G.F. Stidolph, a minor Ipswich builder of organs and pianos, at a cost of £115. The invoice refers simply to 'the organ lately standing in the Corn Exchange, Ipswich'. The original account can be found among the miscellaneous papers of the Halesworth Independent Church – SRO(L)230/6/3 – in the Lowestoft branch of the Suffok Record Office.

3 Newby, J., *Independency in Halesworth & District*, 1936, p92.

Harvey, therefore, must have sensed that what he was doing would upset some of the church members. But he cannot have anticipated the full force of the storm which now broke, the ten years of unseemly bickering, charging and counter-charging, which possessed the life of all Congregationalists in this little town. None of the participants were to come out of it particularly well. When all was done it would appear to have been 'an inglorious affair'.

1866

It was on 28 October 1866 that the Minister, the Rev. Henry Coleman,[4] announced to the Church Meeting that:

> A special church meeting will be held next Thursday evening at half past seven to decide whether the *Gloria* should be sung regularly in our worship on the Lord's day.

The minutes of that special meeting do not, alas, record the arguments deployed for and against the *Gloria*. They simply indicate that George Haward,[5] a deacon of Baptist background, persuaded the church that

> The words of the *Gloria* are an appropriate expression of Praise to the Holy Trinity, but it is not expedient to continue these as a form of worship.

The spark was small but it had been struck. The touch-paper burned and the resulting explosion was to blow the whole place apart. It may seem extraordinary that the 30 words of the short *Gloria* had the power to divide this Halesworth Independent congregation and keep it split for a decade and more. But this is what occurred. Was it a matter of principle, of deeply held conviction or of deeply felt dislike? Was it about prejudice or belief? Was it only a pretext for a conflict between persons which had long been waiting to erupt?

The argument spilled over into the pages of the *Halesworth Times* whose letter columns reflected, week after week, the intensity of the affair.[6] The organist himself revealed that he had introduced the *Gloria*

> at the repeated request of a great many persons, both members of the Church, of the choir, and of the congregation at large; and I did not consider it right to drop it simply to meet the views of some half-dozen individuals...My firm conviction is that prejudice has had more to do with the opposition to the *Gloria* than anything else, except perhaps a spirit of obstinacy...In my own case, and that of many others, the use of the *Gloria* has tended to increase the spirituality of the worship, and to elevate the soul to greater heights of devotion.[7]

Harvey had no doubt it was the obstinacy of the senior deacon that had created the rift. This was confirmed in a letter from 'one in constant

4 Rev. H. Coleman (1809-1882), Newport Pagnell Academy; Minister at Wickhambrook, Suffolk; at Halesworth since 1864; later at Penryn, Cornwall.

5 George Haward (1819-?). Brother of Robert and Charles. See Introduction, p14.

6 *Halesworth Times*, December 1866 and January 1867.

7 For a discussion of what might have led Harvey to introduce the *Gloria*, see the Postcript, p75.

attendance since the days of Rev. Dennant, whose memory still smells sweet and blossoms in the dust'[8]:

> The Baptist element in the Independent Church will be its ruin. Why, Sir, the head deacon is a Baptist and many of the principal members are of the same persuasion, aided by a few narrow-minded individuals...There is a Baptist Church in the town, with a respectable minister at its head. Why do they not go there? It is, I think, just as incongruous for a Baptist to be Deacon of an Independent Church as it is for a Dissenter to be a Churchwarden...

1866-7

Whereupon George's brother Charles,[9] himself for some years a Baptist, wrote supporting neither Harvey's innovation nor George's obstinacy. Charles suggested that 'the new forms [such as the *Gloria*] were but an effort to produce a sort of galvanized life, utterly inefficient for the great ends of Christian union'. The important thing, he wrote, was for the old forms to be life-inspiring. 'Let the prayer, the hymn and the sermon all be pregnant with life'. We shall see that few men could be less life-inspiring than George Haward.

Harvey, too, was a man of very definite views, and the arrogance of his convictions. He would not accept defeat. He now prepared to fight, and many others with him, the battle for a more relaxed Congregationalism. But still, if possible, within his own church:

> *Halesworth Church Book, 25 November*
>
> Mr Harvey read a paper to the meeting showing that George Haward, in what he had stated at the special meeting, had not desired to say anything derogatory as to his [Harvey's] moral and Christian character. Mr Haward made a few conciliatory remarks and left the matter to rest.

The matter did not rest. Such a furious exchange broke out that John Day of Quay Street, printer, bookseller, china dealer and Superintendant of the Sunday School, proposed that a resolution could only be reached if a further special meeting was held. Samuel Brown countered that such a meeting was 'inexpedient'. When the vote was taken, forty voted with Brown, only fourteen with John Day. Six weeks later on 3 January 1867 Harvey tendered his resignation as organist. They tried to tempt him back:

> *Halesworth Church Book, 27 January*
>
> Mr Harvey was asked unanimously to resume his kind offices at the organ. He made a somewhat lengthened speech and concluded by making conditions of his playing which the Pastor decided should not be put to the meeting. In the circumstances Mrs Sheldrake, Miss Coleman and Miss Susannah Haward were invited to preside at the organ until more suitable arrangements could be made.

8 The good Mr Dennant had left in 1840.

9 Charles Haward (1815-1895), Bramfield farmer, temperamentally at the opposite pole to his brother George. See Introduction, p14.

Pastor Coleman's refusal to put Harvey's propositions (whatever they were) to the meeting caused him a good deal of trouble. During the winter there was a whispering campaign against him in the town and protesting letters were exchanged. Three deacons and 78 members supported the pastor's action. But one deacon and 29 members called on him to resign. Where did his duty lie?

1867

Halesworth Church Book, 26 May
The minister said that so long as he was sustained by the majority he dare not desert the post, however painful and trying it might become...Whilst he could never bow to the dictum of a faction he would be ready and quick to listen to the voice of the church when that voice was legitimately and fairly uttered. The coexistence of two antagonistic ruling powers in the same community was a palpable absurdity...such a state of things could only be productive of conflict, disaster and ruin.

The Meeting's anger then turned on the dissidents. They were accused of harbouring a spirit of injustice and cruelty towards 'our Pastor', of uniting themselves for the purpose of breaching Church Authority, of keeping up an 'injurious state of agitation' in the Church. Peace would never be restored as long as they continued their 'confederated action'. By 46 to 20 votes the Meeting 'solemnly and earnestly' required Harvey and his supporters to 'disband'.

A further Church Meeting on 9 June heard that seven of the eight dissident leaders had sent letters 'not by any means complying with the request of the church'. Harvey as usual had the most direct thing to say: 'I refuse to promise that which is required of me'. The resulting chaos was such that the meeting was adjourned until 20 June. But that further meeting was no better, Harvey admitting quite openly that chaos was being caused deliberately:

Halesworth Church Book, 20 June
...attempts were made by some of the insubordinate members to create disorder...Mr Harvey especially persisted in introducing irrelevant matters and asserted that he and his seven brethren had determined that no business should be done if he were not permitted to speak.

S. Brown and G. Haward moved that the leading dissidents be suspended from fellowship until they are led to see and acknowledge their error in refusing to submit to the decisions of the church.

W. Aldred and J. Harvey moved that inasmuch as no brother has committed any act of moral deliquency, or has been charged with doctrinal heresy, this church does not desire that any of its members be suspended.

The vote went against the dissidents 51 to 36.

The moment the result was announced Mr Aldred loudly declared that he and Mrs Aldred withdrew their membership. So did the other leaders.

Thereupon the meeting moved to suspend Harvey and his followers from the 'fellowship of the Church'. No sense of order remained. The noise and disturbance was so great that it was impossible to put the original proposition. *1867-8*
The minister then declared the meeting to be dissolved and retired.

Thirty one members were ejected from the Quay Street Church on that day. The eight leaders were Joseph Harvey, schoolmaster; William Aldred, grocer; John Day, printer and stationer; John Gostling, chemist; Stephen Hadingham, miller; Alfred Long, inland revenue officer; Samuel Smith, coach builder; and Josiah Waller, private resident.

They were followed by Mrs Smith, Mrs Waller, Mrs Gostling, Mrs Day, Mrs Hadingham, Mrs Harvey, Miss Bloomfield, Charles Haward,[10] Samuel Eade, Henry Cornish and Sarah Cornish, C.A. Bicker and Miss Bicker, N.A.Taylor, Mrs Rackham senior, Mrs Rackham junior, Mrs Sewell, Mrs Long and Miss Long, Mrs Burne, Mrs Aldred, Mrs Mannall and Mr Lunnis. On 27 October members voted that those names should be erased from the Church Book.

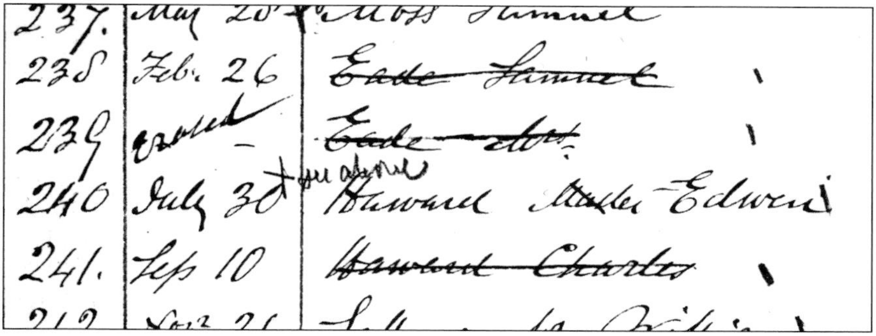

238	Feb. 26	Eade Samuel
239		Eade ditto
240	July 30	Haward Walter Edwin
241.	Sep 10	Haward Charles

Halesworth United Reformed Church

Those ejected withdrew, went up the hill to Harvey's residence at Castle House and formed a breakaway church. With one or two exceptions, it would be ten years before they returned.

Six months later the Church was told of seven further members – Messrs Cage, Hurren,Took, Wigg, Read, W. Etheridge and Ann Etheridge – 'who so far sympathised with the separists [sic] as to abstain from communing and worshipping with us'. Their names also were 'taken from the Church Book'.

At first the new church found it difficult to find a permanent home for themselves. In November the *Halesworth Times* announced a 'series of penny-readings being held in a large workshop opposite the Quay' with

10 Not one of the Bramfield Hawards. He was a builder of Barrack Yard, Bridge Street.

Harvey as one of the readers. But within a few months the dissidents had attracted such support that they moved to the Assembly Room[11] in the centre of town where, it was announced, a 'Public Tea Meeting of the New Congregational Church' was to take place. George Rackham, editor of the *Halesworth Times*, whose wife was a member, wrote in March 1868 that 'from the great success which has attended the ministrations of this body it is expected that a large number will be present at this their first public meeting'.

1868

Such support encouraged the new Church to feel confident enough to search for and engage a young pastor of its own. He was a virile candidate, possibly without formal training:

Halesworth Times, 7 April

> We understand that Mr Richard A. Cliff[12] of Woolwich has accepted a cordial and unanimous invitation from the members of the new congregational church to become their first pastor and will enter upon the duties of his office on the third sabbath of the present month.

The 21-year-old Rev. Richard Athol Cliff's opening service took place as advertised, Joseph Harvey playing the organ. We assume they sang the *Gloria*.

Six months later Pastor Coleman, exhausted by the battle and after only four years in Halesworth, announced that he had accepted an invitation from the Congregational Church at Penryn in Cornwall. Hitherto he had been known as a vigorous and successful minister, but he seems to have mishandled the Halesworth troubles from the start. A few weeks later he had gone. When, on 5 October, he wrote to his church in farewell he spoke with pained regret of 'the fiery ordeal through which you as a church and I as your Pastor have been called to pass...and the wicked designs and malicious efforts of those who became hostile to me because I conscientiously stood with you in resisting their sinful confederated attempts to break down and trample underfoot the authority of the Church'.

The Church replied on 18 October, 'we rejoice at your deliverance from the malice of those who have not ceased to persecute you...those who have sought to vilify your character as a shield to their own wickedness'.[13]

Such, even among the most virtuous, is the language of schism.

11 On weekdays the Assembly Room, behind the Angel Inn, reverted to its role as Corn Hall, Courtroom and Ballroom. See p40.

12 Rev. R.A. Cliff (1846-1921). Halesworth 1868, Walpole, Harleston, King's Lynn, Grantham, Hunstanton. The *Congregational Year Book* of 1922 remarked that he was 'a preacher of rare quality and his conduct of public worship was singularly beautiful'.

13 These two letters are to be found tucked away among the books deposited in the Suffolk Record Office at Lowestoft.

Rev. Richard Athol Cliff, venerable and respected in later life, was radical and controversial in his first pastorates at Halesworth and Walpole.

Union Church, Hunstanton

Norfolk Record Office (FC35/8)

Cliff in his 30s at a meeting of the Norfolk Congregational Union at Harleston where he was pastor.

Yours very truly
John Browne

2
MEDIATION
1868–1869

There now enters the substantial presence of the Reverend John Browne, Secretary of the Eastern Suffolk Congregational Union and pastor of the Independent Church at Wrentham, a few miles to the north.[14] With the old church for the moment without a pastor, Browne tried to negotiate a settlement. In December 1868 he wrote to the Quay Street deacons suggesting they should try to reconcile their differences with the breakaway church. They replied, a touch cheekily, that they were happy to show him their Church Book for examination and if he had any proposition towards a solution would he please put it on paper for their consideration.

Nobody addressed John Browne in that manner and got away with it. He was a force in Suffolk Congregationalism which was hard to resist. He was just completing his exhaustive *History of Congregationalism in Norfolk and Suffolk* which, 130 years later, still maintains a high reputation for accuracy and scholarship. He knew better than most about the vagaries and mishaps of Suffolk nonconformity. He addressed George Haward, Senior Deacon, in a magisterial style worthy of a Trollopian archdeacon:

> *Browne to George Haward, 21 December*
> I am much obliged to you for your letter and though it did not go the length which I could have desired I submitted it to Mr Flower[15] and we both agreed it would be well for the church with which you are connected to resolve the present difficulties before they proceed to the important duty of electing a minister. They should declare their willingness to receive such of the seceding members as are willing to return in a spirit of Christian love and co-operate with them as aforetime in the advancement of the Redeemer's Kingdom. We think it the least you can do under the circumstances to intimate that the door is open and to shew your readiness to receive those who are willing voluntarily to return – such an act on their part might be considered a tacit acknowledgement that they had

14 Rev. John Browne (1823-1886), University College, London, and Coward College; minister at Wrentham for 37 years from 1849. For decades he dominated the Suffolk Union. A preacher of 'Cromwellian force'.

15 Rev. John Flower (1809-1881), Highbury. Minister at Beccles since 1837. Attended opening service at Quay Street in 1836. Close colleague of John Browne in the Suffolk Congregational Union.

taken a wrong course – and I do not know that I should advise you to insist on any other conditions.

1869

The Halesworth church's reply was dismissive. Although they expressed 'deep respect' for the suggestion of their Ministerial Brethren, they felt that, having the 'safety of the Church's peace at heart', they could not advise the Church to take any initiary step. They would simply wait for any personal applications from seceding members who might wish to return.

Negotiating with the hard-liners of Quay Street was going to be difficult. One observer, however, thought they were behaving like angels. After the annual tea meeting of the Quay Street Church, on 25 February, the Suffolk Congregational Union Journal[16] reported that 'the Halesworth Church is full of peace; a spirit of prayer and harmony apparently prevails'.

It is interesting that Browne had chosen to wait more than a year and not to get involved in this affair, despite its seriousness, until after Coleman had departed. Was he somewhat wary of the man? Five years earlier, when Browne had preached at the Recognition and Induction of Coleman at Halesworth he had prefaced his remarks with these words: 'I feel it would be an impertinence for me, a younger brother[17] in the ministry, to attempt to offer any instructions to one who has already been so many years in office…'. The words could simply be a courtesy, but one senses that there was more to them.

Something else had happened at that Induction service which certainly had offended the deacons and congregation of Quay Street. During his address Browne had uttered some stringent criticisms of the 'negligent' way Congregational churches remunerated their ministers:

> Our deacons generally have no clear and definite knowledge of what their pastors actually require. They content themselves with some general notions of what is necessary. There are those who pay £20, £40 or £60 a year for the education of their children, who think as many shillings a quarter a bountiful sum to subscribe towards the costs of the spiritual teacher of the whole family.

This must have elicited some sharp reactions. For when Browne submitted the text of his address for publication as a pamphlet[18] he added an appendix. It was partly an apology that some might have thought he had been criticising those present, whereas Browne argued that he had only been 'sowing a few seeds'. Nonetheless he reinforced his original point by adding, 'let the principal members of each congregation feel that this is their business'.

16 A few issues of this short-lived journal are held by the Norfolk Studies Library, Norwich.
17 Browne was 14 years younger than Coleman.
18 Published by John Day, Quay Street, Halesworth, 1864. Colman Collection, Norfolk Studies Library.

We shall see that Browne was never accepted by the deacons of Quay Street as a genuine arbitrator. Were they still smarting at the memory of his words to them five years before?

1869

For whatever reason, Quay Street flouted Browne's advice and went straight ahead with appointing a new pastor. He was the Rev. Abraham Jackson[19] from Wickham Market. If he had any ideas of leading a quiet and satisfying life in Halesworth, he was soon disabused. The indefatigible figure of Edward Grimwade,[20] Chairman of Browne's Suffolk Congregational Union came into sight. Grimwade was already coming to Jackson's Induction. And he was coming to bring the senior Halesworth church into line. In advance of the day he wrote this firm but understanding letter to the new man about what was expected of his church.

> *Grimwade to Jackson, Norton House, Ipswich, 25 May*
> I have been thinking much of Thursday next[21] and I wonder what has been done by you and your friends to the seceders from your place. Not only what has been done but what can be done. I grieve over the division. It is not for the honour of our Master and Lord but against him and his cause that these things operate. I do not know what you have done, but I say carefully, thoughtfully, kindly and prayerfully: seek to do the right thing, in the right way and at the right time to heal the division. And I pray that your friends may have the honour of taking the first step, and that such a step as will receive from the Master a 'well done'.
>
> I hope to be with you on Thursday in good time in the morning. I shall come from Beccles, whither I go on Wednesday night by the last train, and shall be glad to see you at the station if you have any word to say to me.

Did Jackson meet Grimwade at the station and explain during their five minute walk to the chapel how intransigent his new flock were? We do not know. But in the railway compartment going home to Ipswich after the service Grimwade clearly talked hard with his clerical companion about the likely outcome. On reaching home he wrote once again to Jackson:

> *Grimwade to Jackson, 28 May*
> I had a long chat with Mr. Reeve[22] on my way home this morning. Mr R agrees with me that what you intend will not do. It will only add fuel to

19 Rev. Abraham Jackson (1816-1881), came from Wickham Market 1869, moved to Debenham 1876.

20 Edward Grimwade (1812-1886), tailor and outfitter and Mayor-elect of Ipswich. He was the most energetic lay force in the Suffolk Congregational Union at this time.

21 The day of Jackson's induction, 28 May 1869.

22 Rev. Jonah Reeve, Congregational Minister at Stowmarket since 1858; a member of the Suffolk Union's executive committee.

> the fire. I am sure your thought and future action...is to exhibit the Spirit of your Lord and Master. Pray execute your influence to carry a resolution somewhat like the enclosed. I pray a hearty blessing may abide upon the past day.

1869

Grimwade's enclosure read thus:

> ...this church, anxious to be guided by the Spirit of the Divine Master and deeply conscious of our common affirmities, desire to forget the past and will rejoice to welcome the separated brethren back to its fellowship, to work unitedly and earnestly for him who died to reconcile us to God.

On the same day, Browne added his own plea in a letter to Jackson:

> Do all you can to favour the arrangement and let us hope & pray that some way may be found out of the entanglement.

If there was urgency in the situation, Jackson did not succeed in conveying it to his deacons. Four weeks went by before they took up the matter. And then they resolved to answer the Union in the following terms:

> *Halesworth Church Book, 1 July*
> Having well considered your resolution we must express our conviction that the cause of Christ will be better advanced by standing still and leaving those parties time for reflection.

Having stubbornly opposed John Browne, the deacons had now rejected the advice of their own new minister, if Jackson had in fact done the Union's bidding. Browne, thoroughly roused by this time, had clearly expected Jackson to perform miracles:

> *Browne to Jackson, 6 July*
> ...I want you to look at the question in this light. We know that nothing has been done in Halesworth in consequence of my last communication. It was practically a dead letter. Anxious to destroy the scandal which affects the whole body of the church...we are willing to investigate the causes with a view to healing it. Overtures have been made to both parties. If either party declines it will greatly weaken its moral position. I personally think (and this note is personal and not official) that your friends will damage their cause if they show a disinclination to concur in the arrangement...You are not to conclude that you must reunite at any risk. You may conclude that under present circumstances you should stand apart, in which case they may recommend that the Union should provisionally recognise the other party – this I do not know. But I do fear that if your friends determine to sit still and decline this proposition and the others accept it, it will be injurious to you...

The Pastor replied four days later that his church's views were unchanged, and chided Browne for his petulance. And he issued a counter-warning which went right to the roots of Independency, that each Church should decide for itself how it should manage its affairs:

'Something had to be done' about the schism in Halesworth. Among the mediators was the Ipswich tailor Edward Grimwade, chairman of the Suffolk Congregational Union, and a temperate foil to his Secretary, Rev. John Browne of Wrentham.

Jackson to Browne, 10 July

1869

> I believe there are fundamental principles of our Independency involved in this matter; and if the action which seems to be shadowed out in the communications we have received were carried out I fear it would be most disastrous to the peace, the order, the prosperity and the security of our Independent Churches.

Browne writes quickly back to still Jackson's indignation:

Browne to Jackson, 12 July

> My last was not official, neither is this...I quite see your difficulty – but I can assure you that nothing is further from the wish of the Committee than to interfere unconstitutionally, their great object being to abate the scandal arising out of the schism.

Browne must have wondered when the agony was going to end. In fact, it was only just beginning.

For months past, Harvey had been trying to obtain official recognition for his breakaway New Church. Since the 1830s, Congregationalism had argued about the very point which Abraham Jackson had put so forcibly to Browne: individual churches might need the support of Congregational Unions in raising funds to keep the cause alive. But such organisations inevitably grow to wield considerable power and attract much suspicion and resentment. Independents had come into existence specifically to escape powerful men who liked nothing more than telling those beneath them what to do and how to do it.

Harvey had all the 'independence' he could wish for, but somehow not the respect. He had broken away from an established fold. What his church needed – and he personally – was a shepherdly pat on the head, a fatherly gesture of acceptance, an official recognition of status. The Suffolk Union had firmly told him that such things were not to be his. 'All separation', they said, 'save in cases of extreme necessity, is opposed to the Law of the Lord Jesus Christ'.

When Browne and Grimwade once again urged both sides to go to arbitration and so heal the split, Harvey's party had said it was willing. But, once again, the senior church would not budge.

Despite this Harvey held out what seemed to be an olive branch. He wrote to Pastor Jackson on 9 September inviting him to their Harvest Home Tea Meeting in the Assembly Room –'We shall be glad if you will favour us with your presence and take a part in the evening's proceedings'. Jackson's gentle reply perhaps suggests that he did not altogether share the hard line which his committee went on instructing him to adopt:

It will perhaps be sufficient for me to insinuate that the circumstances between yourselves and us are very peculiar, and my presence might be misunderstood. With best wishes for the spiritual prosperity of the church.

1869

Jackson would not be at the party. But the *Halesworth Times* reporter seemed not to be aware of this. After the event, he wrote that Jackson had been among the speakers. He must have known that there would have been severe trouble in Quay Street if their pastor had been discovered offering any comfort to the junior church. So what was he up to? Was he incompetent or deceitful? He also reported that Grimwade took the chair. Had Harvey gulled the Chairman of the Suffolk Union into believing that Jackson would be present, thus making the 30-mile train journey from Ipswich worthwhile? Deviousness was certainly among Harvey's skills and he may have been exercising it here:

Halesworth Times, 20 September

A public tea took place at half-past five, when some 500 guests sat down to a bountiful spread. After tea, a public meeting was held under the presidency of Edward Grimwade Esq., Mayor of Ipswich. Eloquent discourses were also delivered by Mr R. Haward (Mells Hill),[23] the Revs. Dr Salisbury[24] (Cratfield), C. Carey[25] (Bungay), A. Jackson (Halesworth), and R. A. Cliff (pastor of the Free Congregational Church).The evening meeting was densely crowded, numbers being unable to gain admittance into the Hall.

Still thwarted in his campaign for recognition, Harvey resumed his letter-writing. Most of these letters display a flamboyant self-importance which can aggravate the most understanding reader. He and his colleagues no doubt had a justifiable case to put, but one is left wondering if an occasional touch of 'Christian' modesty might not have been more persuasive. Now he had spotted another slight. He complained to Browne that he had not put forward their new Church for inclusion in the national Congregational Year Book:

Harvey to Browne, 29 October

I assume we are in the same position as Cratfield...they are not in official communication with the Suffolk Congregational Union, neither are we. Upon what ground shall that church be returned for the Year Book and

23 Robert Haward, (1813-1884), brother to Charles and George. Walpole Chapel trustee. See Introduction p14.

24 Rev Dr J.C. Salisbury (1805-1889), minister at Cratfield, near Halesworth, since 1861.

25 Rev. Charles Stokes Carey (1828-1875), Bassingbourne, Harwich, Bungay (1860-1871), then Leytonstone. Close colleague of John Browne's in the Suffolk Congregational Union.

> ours omitted?...As you are frequently in Halesworth the existence of our church can be evidenced by your calling upon me, when I can show you the necessary documents. It is not that we attach any great importance to the insertion of our Church and Pastor in the Year Book etc. But we are determined to assert our right to the various privileges connected with our position as a church, and leave the responsibility of refusal upon those with whom we are thus brought into contact.

1869

Browne's reply is missing, but he must have fired back immediately because only three days later Harvey is writing at even greater length and with even more self-justifying passion:

> *Harvey to Browne, 1 November*
>
> I note yr remark in your favour that it is no pleasure to you to be 'brought into antagonism with me'. I fully reciprocate the sentiment; it has been one of the most painful elements of the strife I have been forced to pass through that I have been 'brought into antagonism' with ministers and other gentlemen with whom I had for many years been on terms of friendliness and intercourse. It has however been a strong comfort to me to have the firm and calm conviction that I have done nothing to merit the passive coldness of some and the active antagonism of others...I put it to you as a Xn[26] man, taking a common sense view of matters: if you had been driven from your own sanctuary, mainly by Baptists, formed a church and taken half the congregation with you and turned adrift into the world, honourable return barred, what do you do but with your friends organise another sphere of Xn activity, & provide the means of the worship of God for those who sympathised with you? Were we who were Nonconformists by principle and practice to go over to the Ch of England in a body, or to cease the public worship of God altogether?

Once again no record of how Browne replied. But before many days are out Harvey resumes in full spate:

> *Harvey to Browne, 13 November*
>
> Your letter of the 9th forms no answer to mine of 1st inst – the chief portion of it being wholly irrelevant to our case...we on our side resisted the partition of the church as far as we possibly could. The other side determined that there should be separation. Yet we are stigmatised as the separatists, and are made to bear both the odium and the disadvantages, as though we had been the cause of the separation...Every custom of the Church at Halesworth, acted upon through a long series of years, was set at nought by the minister and his party...We were driven from our sanctuary, hallowed to us by the worship of our fathers & ourselves for a long course of years. We were persecuted for the truth and for righteousness' sake. And when we looked on the right hand and on the left, 'no man cared for our souls', at least no man of the neighbouring congr. churches, lay or cleric. We asked advice, and got none, but to arbitrate,

26 As many of these letters demonstrate, the sign of the Cross was an accepted way of indicating the name of Christ.

which our opponents refused. We asked help and sympathy & got only cold neglect...Were we to go to Church, or else to neglect public worship meanwhile?...It is easy for you to sit at home at your ease (ecclesiastically) and from the Secretary's chair just to say 'I should not have done as you did'. Pray, what could be done, except perhaps to 'return and acknowledge our error', when we were not, and are not yet conscious of having committed any error, to confess to our equally & more erring brethren?

1869

As to the Union, again, what have we got for our pains? 'Go back' says the Union to us & 'silence the old church fraternally'. And the Diotrephes[27] of the old church tells us you must return as penitents, as coming from the world. Then the Committee of the Union proposes arbitration; we accept, they reject it. Yet no sympathy, only blame. Solemnly we say it 'The Lord judge between you and us'. God does not, for purposes we cannot fathom, always cause the right to prosper. Hitherto He has blessed us, & that abundantly, us and our beloved young Pastor, far beyond our most sanguine expectation.

The other side determined that there sh'd be separation. Yet we are stigmatized as the separatists, and are made to bear both the odium and the disadvantage, as though we had been the cause of the separation.

Harvey's hand – in his usual emphatic style. *SRO, Ipswich*

While Harvey was venting his anger on Browne the 'old church' had been drafting an invitation to the 'new' to return to the fold. At first sight, disregarding all the pompous archaisms, it seems to convey a warm, friendly and forgiving message. Perhaps at last there had been a change of heart. But no, it was the smile on the face of the tiger:

Text of letter from the Halesworth Church Book, 9 November

The Church of Christ assembling at the Independent Chapel Halesworth to those Brethren who seceded from our fellowship Sendeth Greetings. Whereas the present division existing among the Independents of this town is a scandle [sic] and a reproach upon our common Christianity. Whereas we believe the cause of the Redeemer generally would be honoured and better served by a hearty reconciliation; whereas the subject of the *Gloria* was the immediate cause of the trouble; whereas much bitterness was expressed in reference to individuals; whereas the Great Principle of Church Government by the voice of the majority was at stake which was the ultimate cause of the separation; whereas intimations have been heard by us from time to time as individuals, though not officially, that you are willing to return to our midst and are searching and longing for some word from us; whereas there appears to be a doubt in your

27 The reference is to the third Epistle of *John*, vv 9-10, where John censures Diotrephes for 'prating against us with malicious words'.

> minds as to whether or not we would receive you back to our fellowship; whereas there are individuals who have joined your fellowship since the time of your secession from us.

1869

> Therefore it seemeth good to us to send you the following inclinations in order to achieve a reunion:
>
> 1. Be it mutually agreed to put away from our heart, and never more to mention the former ill feelings and divergences of heart and mind in reference to this matter;
>
> 2. Be it mutually agreed that the question of the *Gloria*, as the ostensible beginning of the disruption, be considered a matter finally settled by the Church;
>
> 3. Be it mutually agreed that persons who have joined your fellowship since your secession from us can be received only in the usual course of Church order, namely a visitation by delegates appointed by this Church;
>
> 4. Be it mutually agreed that Mr Harvey be invited to resume his office at the Organ and eligible for re-election as Deacon;
>
> 5. Be it mutually agreed that Mr Day, and those formally engaged in the School, be invited to co-operate therein;
>
> 6. Be it *acknowledged and regretted on your part by your signifying assent to this paper that you did wrong in the sight of God, and to this Church, by resisting and withstanding its unmistakeable decisions, and in your continued agitation afterwards.*[28]

If the Church in the Assembly Room wished to return to Quay Street it would have to crawl.

28 The italics are mine.

Halesworth & District Museum

All that was left, in the 1960s, of the Assembly Room where Harvey's New Congregational Church met. It later became a cinema, then was demolished.

3
CONFUSION
1870

Browne and his fellow ministers tried yet again to find a workable solution to the Halesworth problem. For years Browne had been one of those in the Congregational Union encouraging the older, smaller, often remoter, churches with diminishing congregations to amalgamate with those which had been springing up in the towns. The 'gathered' congregation at Walpole, in the countryside two miles out of Halesworth, was one of these. Formed out of the white heat of the Civil War, surviving and thriving despite persecution and privation, it was now little more than a distinguished relic. As it happened, the Pastor at Walpole, H. J. Haas,[29] had played into Browne's hands. Haas seems to have been involved in local talk about the young deacon's wife, Mary Seaman, who was also church organist. If he could be given an honourable way out by resigning, it might be possible to persuade Walpole to accept Cliff as their new man. If that were to work, Walpole might be revived and the troublesome seceding church in Halesworth could be dissolved. Some of Cliff's congregation might follow him to Walpole, others would individually become reunited with the Quay Street church. In the spring of 1870 Browne apparently wrote to Robert Haward, the senior of the trio of brothers and a Walpole trustee, to let the him know what was planned. But, as so often, Browne did not reveal the whole plan. So Haward had to write back asking for some flesh on the bones:

> *Robert Haward to Browne, Mells Hill, 16 May*
>
> I have been unusually busy or your favour of the 7th would not have been so long unanswered. Before placing the Walpole Chapel, and the property with which it is endowed, entirely in the hands of the [Suffolk Congregational] Union my father[30] and the trustees would like to be in possession of the scheme which will then have to be drawn up for the management of the old place. They will favourably look upon any project that may be placed before them and I will with pleasure, on a future occasion, convene a meeting of them, and either introduce you or bring myself the matter before them.

29 H.J. Haas (1805-1880), Minister at West Mersea, Essex; Nayland, Suffolk; Crediton, Devon; Walpole since 1856. He received only a brief obituary in the *Congregational Year Book* of 1881.

30 Robert Haward (1790-1875), born in Cookley, baptised at Walpole; Bramfield farmer. Father of the three Haward brothers, see Introduction p14. A former trustee of Walpole Chapel. He donated land for Bramfield Chapel, built opposite his own house.

And Haas, sensing that something more was meant than had been said to him by Browne, also wanted some reassurance:

1870

Haas to Browne, Walpole, 23 May

With regard to your proposition: before I signify my intention to resign and commit my surviving flock (though comparatively small, beloved, persecuted, united and faithful) to your guidance, which in ordinary circumstances I should have been glad to do, you must give me some idea of what you propose to do for them. Will you favour me with the appointment of an interview for conference upon the subject. Our late friend Alexander[31] once said to me, "Walpole (ie the Trustees) is the *ne plus ultra*". He was right, knowing, as he evidently did, the experiences of Wearing, Mayhew & Lewis [Haas's three predecessors at Walpole]. I quote from the *English Independent*, "Your Lordships may darn till doomsday, but you never can make freeholds and spirituality hang together". [32]

Two months went by. Robert Haward urges John Browne to hurry things along:

Robert Haward to Browne, 19 July

As soon as you have made any arrangement about Walpole I will call on Mr Moore[33] the old deacon of the church to summon a meeting of the members and have no doubt but they will sanction it. Mr Haas is gone and I do not know who has supplied the pulpit for the last 2 Sundays, but I hope you will take steps to send a minister directly. I will see Mr Cliff to-day as if he accepts the office he may register immediately.

The absence of Cliff from Walpole may have been to do with the parallel negotiations which Browne and his colleagues had been conducting with the Assembly Room church. The text we have is only a sketch:

Flower, Browne and C. Stokes Carey to Rev. R.A. Cliff [undated]

We beg to call yr attention to follg statements re Walpole...Minister of this Ch Rev. H.J. Haas, having at our instance obtained a pension... trustees and chapel have agreed to acquiesce in any arrangements which we think it right to make...Chapel at Walpole has an endowment of £50 pr ann & an excellent minister's house. The cause is at present very low but we know no reason why it shld not flourish once more. Shd you consent to doing so we are prepared to recommend to friends at Walpole

31 Probably Rev. John Alexander, celebrated minister of Prince's Street Congregational Chapel, Norwich, from 1817 to 1866. Died 1868.

32 Walpole's muscular independence was firmly established. It had since the late seventeenth century owned a good deal of local property and in 1849 had built a handsome manse for its pastor. Haas's words refer to Walpole's reputation of seeming to care more for its rental income than for the spiritual wellbeing of its members.

33 William Moore (1793-1878) a deacon of Walpole Chapel for at least twenty years. Farmed 42 acres at nearby Peasenhall. His gravestone is in the chapel ground at Walpole.

> to receive you as pastor, *provided only that both you and your people agree to dissolve the ch over which you at present preside.*[34] As many as would prefer to do so cd then become members of the ch at Walpole...many others would I have no doubt be received into the old church at Halesworth under our mediation...We believe yr friends are so attached to you that many would accompany you to Walpole – we have only this to say: if you choose to hold a service on Sunday evening at H, to do so will be inconsistent with this arrangement. Therefore we do wish you to have remembrance of the unseemly strife, which must not be be perpetuated. Whatever may be just now, we are certain that in the long run Halesworth cannot sustain two flourishing Independent causes, and therefore we are profoundly convinced that it is to the glory of God if every appearance of disharmony is done away. Will you kindly take these suggestions into prayerful consideration and also bring them before your people?

1870

A jotting separated from the text says:

> I do say very sincerely that we are deeply sorry for the necessity which requires any interruption of the relations in which your people stand with yourself.

A note from Flower shows that Browne had included the last few words at the urging of his colleague. Flower says:

> You see our great difficulty is that the people will think we are ready to deprive them of religious ordinances in our determination to carry our point. Cliff begged me to communicate with him as soon as possible after we had agreed on a letter as he is greatly excited about this matter. So please send it on by first post if it meets your wishes.

Once the letter reached him, Cliff did what he was asked. But it was Harvey who replied to Browne and his colleagues. It began to look as if this was a scheme which might actually work:

> *Harvey to Browne, 27 June*
>
> At a meeting of the Pastor and Committee of the New Congregational Church of this town, held this evening, it is agreed, subject to the approval of that Church, that Mr Cliff should go to Walpole, provided an honourable arrangement can be made for our re-union with the Church in Quay Street...This we do, at your suggestion, for the sake of peace and harmony, and shall be ready to confer with the representatives of that church, in conjunction with yourselves, upon definite terms, as soon as they are willing thus to meet us in the matter.

But we learn from Browne, in this note to Flower, that his plans were not going well. If Walpole and the Assembly Room were compliant, things in Quay Street were unchanged:

34 The italics are mine.

Browne to Flower, 24 July

1870

Carey suggests that I write at once to Jackson and ask whether the old party will enter into treaty with the seceders (through us) on this basis: 1. The seceders who wish to join to be received en masse; 2. All offensive pages to be expunged (under our supervision) from the Church Book. If so, then both parties to meet with us – I added that if they preferred to do so we could meet with them alone first as we had done with the others – I put the case very strongly to them and urged them in the Master's name to do every thing to abate and remove the scandal. I urged it also in the name of the Church of this county. The reply I have received this morning.

[The reply read as follows:
I am requested to forward the following resolution passed at the Committee Meeting last evening. 'The Committee appointed by the Independent Church Halesworth, having seriously considered the suggestion contained in the Revd J. Browne's letter to the Revd Jackson, find it impossible to recommend the Church to accede to these suggestions being convinced that the interest of Christ's cause would not be advanced thereby, but they would be happy to advise the Church to entertain any individual application for Membership according to the usual order of Independent Churches. Praying every blessing may rest upon you and yours'.]

'Browne to Flower' continues:

Shall we ask them to meet us – to confer on the subject and if possible to bring them to better terms? The other party wants to know what to do. Walpole is vacant, waiting for us. Can we suggest to Cliff that he should take the pastorate of the Walpole Church at once and unite his people with them & work the two as at present for a time – ie till something is done; preach morning & evening at Halesworth and afternoon at Walpole getting what help he can for Walpole morning service. This will do away with the two churches, will possibly more speedily set Walpole up, will obviate the necessity of bringing the Halesworth old church to terms, and leave members to drop back again at their pleasure. It will not do all we wanted – there will still be two congregations in Halesworth but that we cannot help.

In reply, John Flower still tried to find a way round the impasse.

Flower to Browne, 25/27 July

It would only be fair and proper that, in returning, the disaffected party should engage to drop the former feud and in all things seek to please the church which they are rejoining.This should be stated to the old church. Perhaps if they have not confidence in each other now they would not have confidence whatever engagement might be made, but the excuse of the old church no doubt will be that they are afraid to take their former brethren back. You ask me to write to Jackson. I will do so.

So Flower went on to write this tough, but understanding, letter to the Quay Street pastor and his deacons:

1870

Flower to Jackson, 6 August

We feel much regret that your resolution seems to close the hope of any union at present. We are unwilling to bear such a message to the associated churches of our county as you refuse to restore such of the brethren as wish to return to the communion of the old church. Perhaps we might say explicitly that in asking you to receive the brethren back we think you have a right to require them to enter into an engagement that they will not revive past disputes and will in all things seek the peace and welfare of the church to which they return. If such an engagement is entered into on their part we do not see how you can adhere to your resolution which proposes to treat them as 'thou that are without'.

We feel that the present is a critical time for Congregationalism in Halesworth, & for interests which we hold yet dearer still; for if the breach be not healed now, untold mischief will be perpetuated to coming generations, and heavy will be the responsibility incurred by those, on whichever side they may be, who insist on impracticable terms of re-union. We are bound to say that both Mr Cliff and the brethren associated with him met our overtures in a christian spirit. In discharging the difficult and delicate duty which, unsought by us, has fallen to our lot, we have not hesitated to speak with all christian freedom and faithfulness to the brethren who have hitherto worshipped separately; and we feel called upon to do the same toward you.

He received this reply:

Dear Sir, *10 August*

We regret you should have understood our last Resolution as closing 'any hope of reunion at present'. You say that you are unwilling to bear such a message to the associated churches 'that we refuse to restore such of the brethren as wish to return'. We beg to say should you be the bearer of such a message it would be entirely incorrect. However critical you may think the present time for Congregationalism in Halesworth we believe it was much more critical when the only governing power in our Churches was set at naught by those on whose behalf you write. We sympathise with you in the difficult task you have undertaken, especially as you know only in part, and assure you in all Chr. faithfulness you are greatly mistaken if you suppose we wish to place any barrier in the way of any right-minded Chr. uniting with us. Trusting the Great Head of the Church will guide and direct the whole, yours in the Bonds of the Gospel.

W.H. Ives,

Acting Secretary of Quay Street Church.[35]

35 Walter Henry Ives, currier, boot and shoe manufacturer, Bridge Street, Halesworth. Deacon; member since 1861; died 1912.

The appearance of a more reasonable tone in this disingenuous letter is due to the relative fluency of Ives's style rather than any softening of attitude.

1870

Meanwhile at Castle House, Harvey, the headmaster, was pressing on with the detail of Browne's plan, apparently unaware that Quay Street was turning it down:

> *Harvey to Browne, 9 August*
>
> I regret on every ground that I was so occupied last week with the re-opening of my school that I was unable to write you then. On Sunday week the 31 ult I preached at Walpole to an increased congn estimated at nearly 100 persons. I afterwards took tea with Mr Seaman,[36] the only remaining deacon, and chatted with him respecting the proposals. He was quite agreeable and indeed anxious for such an arrangement, and believed the people generally would feel the same. Mr Cliff also is willing to attempt the plan proposed.
>
> There are however two little difficulties. Mr Seaman, as Deacon, has "charge" only of the subscriptions[37] of the congregation, which at present are nil. Mr Moore, the surviving trustee, takes or claims to take all the rents which form the endownment. Mr Seaman believes Mr Moore would agree to the above proposals but cannot say how the funds stand. He understood Mr Moore to say that the "estate" is virtually in debt through the dilapidations permitted by the late pastor, wh will necessitate rather a large outlay on the houses etc.
>
> Besides there is the question of the Walpole Trust deed. It would be so much more satisfactory, both as regards the pecuniary part of the affair, and the status of the minister if we could know its whereabouts. Do you know who holds the Trust deed and could you obtain it for us? Of course Mr Cliff could not enter into any definite arrangement, temporary or otherwise, without knowing his position in regard to that document, which might be used to his disadvantage under circumstances when he might least expect it.
>
> Bye the bye you & the Walpole people (or more strictly speaking Mr Seaman) are I find mutually wondering why the other party (Quay Street) has not written. You expected to hear that they were ready to receive direction etc from you as representing the Union. They were expecting to hear what the Union (through you) proposed. I shewed Mr Seaman your position – now you see his…

Inexplicably, it was not until the end of the following month that the bad news from Quay Street percolated through to the Assembly Room.

36 Simon Seaman, carpenter, sole deacon of Walpole chapel at this time.

37 The subscriptions would have been for pew-rents. Their absence might mean that the church had lost its more well-to-do members.

Harvey to Browne, 25 September

Mr Grimwade told us on Friday week that a Committee meeting had been held at his house at which it was reported that the Ch in Quay Street had refused your request to take into consideration any steps for re-union; and Mr G was in consequence the more anxious to come to us, & give us his sympathy.

1870

Flower to Browne, 4 October

I have had a deputation from the Walpole and Halesworth church and have agreed that we will go over soon to settle matters. My proposal is that if this suits you and Mr Carey we should invite the old church [Walpole] to meet us in the Afternoon and then see the Trustees and Deacon of Halesworth with a depn from the seceding church in the evening of the same day.

The Quay Street deacons' minute book records that 'a long conference' with the County Union's sub-committee (Browne, Carey and Flower) did take place on 20 October. It appears to have had some effect. There had been considerable disagreement between two deacons, the strict and newly arrived tax collector, John Bedwell, and the increasingly emollient grocer Samuel Brown, as to what the church's view should actually be. The 'compromise' which emerged did offer a new warmth:

Resolved in Committee, 28 October

This Church having listened to the correspondence relating to the seceding Brethren and to the action taken by the Committee thereon, desired to express its approval of the course adopted, and to assure any of the seceding Brethren who may desire to return, of our cordial and kind reception of their application, anxious only for the peace and prosperity of the Church.

Browne and his fellow-ministers met the New Church as planned, but the following long and hostile letter shows that something must have gone seriously wrong. Perhaps it was that Harvey had changed course and was therefore at loggerheads with Browne from the start of their discussion. It should also be said that when things deteriorated even further, as they did in the following year, Browne would have no excuse for saying he did not know what might be coming:

Harvey to Browne, 27 October

...with reference to the affairs of the Independent Church at Walpole, we hereby do say – that the Revd R.A. Cliff, our respected Pastor, shall be permitted by our Church to become also the Pastor of the Walpole Church, and that the two churches may, for convenience, be styled "The associated churches of Halesworth & Walpole". That the two churches shall, however, be distinct and separate in the election of their respective officers, in the administration of the ordinances and church discipline. That the stipend which the Pastor shall receive from each of these churches shall be a matter of arrangement between the Pastor and each Church. We shall, on the other hand, look for fulfilment of the promise you gave us last time, to give at once to the New Cong Ch: at Halesworth your practical sympathy so far as convenient to you, and in the ensuing spring to cordially recommend the admission of this church separately to the Suff. Cong. Union. It will of course be understood that we send this to you without prejudice to our position as an Independent ch. It is simply a friendly interchange of ideas between you & us.

1870

We are constrained to speak thus plainly because of the attitude assumed towards us generally hitherto, and even at our interview with yourselves on Thursday last. We have on two occasions requested admission to the Suff. Union, and the only response it has as yet given has been propositions designed for our dissolution as a ch. and congn. without the slightest reference to the nature of our position, and the causes of our separate existence. We are told that the multiplication of small churches is undesirable; and to this principle we may all readily subscribe. But it must in practice necessarily be modified by the individual and special circumstances of each case. Otherwise it may happen that the assertion of a principle shall lead to the perpetration of the grossest injustice.

Now when a large secession takes place from a church, followed by full half the congn., and the seceding members seek counsel from the ministers and laymen of the County:- if these will not enquire into the causes of the secession, they certainly have no right to condemn it...The leading men at the Quay St. Ch. without consulting their church have placed obstacles in the way and shewn by their spirit that cordial Xn. reunion is impracticable. We appeal therefore to your Xn. candour and to the sense of justice & courtesy of the associated churches of Suffolk no longer to trifle with us ...

With Xn salutation...

John Browne and his colleagues had difficulty containing themselves:

Carey to Browne, 28 October

The Halesworth letter is insolence run mad. To give them Walpole is all right, to say a word about themselves is all wrong. We are the culprits and they graciously tell us in what terms they will be reconciled to us.

Flower to Harvey, 30 October

We beg to say that we adhere to the terms proposed at our recent meeting, namely that your church should be merged in that of Walpole...We are not at liberty to make other terms, since the express object for which we were appointed was to prevent the premature establishment of a second church if possible by Christian means...our feeling is that we could only attend the ordination of Mr Cliff (whom we recognise most cordially as a brother minister) if it took place at Walpole...We beg to add our firm resolve now to have done with this matter...

Harvey delayed a whole month before replying but his anger was not in the least abated:

Harvey to Browne, 2 December

1870

We must regard your refusal as a departure from your pledged word, which amazes us all...Surely you must know that you cannot by any means prevent the formation of a second ch. in Halesworth for the simple reason that it has already existed for upwards of three years. Its establishment we trust depends more upon God's favour than man's... We would feign believe that you are only too painfully aware that you and we have been made dupes of by the Quay Street church...many good Xns are, we know, anxious for cordial reunion with us but they are overborne and over-ridden by the 'powers that be'...We return our respectful thanks for the trouble you have taken in this matter, albeit it has not been taken with a single eye to Xn understanding but with the express object of rooting us up, if possible by Xn means.

4
CHAOS
1870–1871

Walpole – the pawn in this increasingly acrimonious contest – was meanwhile preparing to receive Cliff as their pastor, if only a tangle of difficulties could be sorted out. The aged William Moore writes – through his son – to his fellow trustee:

William Moore to Robert Haward, Peasenhall, 13 December

In answer to yours of this morning relative to information about Walpole Chapel I cannot give you any definite information relative to the acceptance by Revd R. Cliff of the pastorate of Walpole Church. Mr Cliff has had an official invitation signed by the Deacon & Trustees to accept the charge, but has not given any written decisive answer that I know of, but I think it is generally understood that he will accept…With regard to the repairs of the Chapel and property we are having them done as quickly as we can unfortunately the weather being bad they cannot get on with the ceiling of the Chapel so quickly as we should like but we hope to get the Chapel opened for worship on the first or second Sunday in the new year. Any further information I shall be most happy to give you if I can…

Haward in his turn passes on Moore's letter to John Browne.

Robert Howard to Browne, Mells Hill, 14 December

I am fully satisfied that the cause at Walpole can only be revived by an earnest ministry and by having two full services at the dear old chapel every Lord's day. Any thing short of this will fail; as the congregation in this thinly populated district must to a great extent be made up of farmers and others, who will travel some miles, and who will not come for one service.

The executive committee of the Suffolk Congregational Union, meeting at Grimwade's house in Ipswich, decided to follow Browne's own line and put a cap on the whole enterprise. Enough, they considered, was enough:

Suffolk Union Executive Committee, 16 December

Mr Browne was requested to write to Mr R. Haward in relation to Walpole to urge him to stop the proceedings there, the recommendations of the Committee having been set aside, and an invitation being about to be given to Mr Cliff whilst there is no amalgamation of the churches

Walpole Old Chapel, a generation after these events, and much smarter than it had been. A century later the minister's vestry door had been closed up.

> contemplated – our only object in his becoming pastor at Walpole being that a union of the churches should thereby be effected.

1871 There is no sign of the Suffolk Union's letter to Robert Haward. If it arrived Haward cannot have understood it. Because those in charge at Walpole had some difficulty in seeing why it was taking so long for their new pastor, Richard Athol Cliff, now actively working at the chapel, to be fully recognised. With an air of desperation Robert Haward remarked to Browne that he was 'unable to fathom what was going on'. But he did reveal that there were local anxieties about Cliff's prospects at Walpole.

> *Robert Haward to Browne, 24 February*
> Mr Cliff, as you know, has accepted the call made by the few persons calling themselves the Walpole church and considers himself as their pastor; and Mr Moore and the other trustees do not consider themselves as justified in trying to oust him, especially as Mr Jameson, his uncle, a gentleman who lives in London retired from business, and who is one of the London Wesleyan evangelists, proposes to live in the parsonage house and to assist his nephew in working the village stations which belong to Walpole,[38] and have since Mr Mayhew's[39] time been almost entirely neglected. Mr Moore having explained these matters to me, I wrote Mr Cliff wishing him success in his work...I have had no reply from Mr C. but on Tuesday a long letter came from Mr Harvey enclosing some 10 sheets of paper closely written containing, as I presume, the correspondence which has taken place between your committee and himself. My time is so fully occupied that I dare not go into this matter...and I deem it an ungracious act to interfere with your conduct of the business placed in your hands. I have therefore returned his voluminous correspondence unread.

Three months passed – and still Walpole was no wiser as to the future of its pastor. In May Simon Seaman, the Walpole deacon, wrote to John Browne complaining that despite Cliff's presence at Walpole and his success over the last six months in building up the congregation, ministers were still writing to apply for his job. Could the Union please announce what had happened so that Cliff was saved further bother?

Browne undertook to announce the fact of Cliff's presence at Walpole in the *Independent Examiner* and *Christian World* newspapers.[40] But then he proceeded in his most mystifying style. The Union was clearly determined not to give the Assembly Room Church an independent credibility, but Browne could not bring himself to ask Seaman the key question clearly

38 These out-stations were the neighbouring villages of Heveningham, Huntingfield and Cookley.
39 Rev. Joseph Mayhew was minister from 1822-1850. He is buried at Walpole Chapel.
40 These were national papers circulating among the Congregational community.

and simply: was it Walpole's intention that Cliff should be minister of a new unified church embracing both Walpole and the new Halesworth congregations? Instead, unable to judge what a village carpenter of 1871 might understand, he wrote:

1871

> *Browne to Seaman, 2 June*
>
> We (the Union) do not wish to interfere in your arrangements but as we took steps to secure the vacancy at Walpole and understood from the Walpole friends that they wished us to superintend the arrangements for their settlement, & as we actually, in furtherance of the understood purposes, did take some of the steps in the matter, we think it only right to ask on what terms this union has been effected in order that we may know what course to pursue in the event of any further arrangement being necessary.

Even his own committee minutes put it more clearly, 'the Union are ready to recognise Mr Cliff as Pastor at Walpole and, if desired, to take part in his ordination there'.

Seaman does his best to answer Browne's questions but, never the most assured letter-writer, does not mention the crucial point, probably because he is quite unaware that it *is* crucial.

> *Seaman to Browne, 13 June*
>
> I hardly know what else to say, than I said in my last letter for I thought you knew all the arrangements indeed most of them were of your own suggesting. You remember when we met you at the King William last Autumn that we were all anxious for Mr Cliff to become our Pastor, and said we must be satisfied with his preaching to us on the Sabbath afternoon, the friends at Halesworth said they could not give him up for the morning, and really it is hardly worth while for a minister to come then, for the attendance is very small, seldom above forty or fifty, but Mr Cliff does come both parts of the day once a quarter as he will do next Sabbath Day; The afternoon congregations are much better than they were last year, sometimes over three hundred. Mr Cliff also conducts the Thursday evening Prayer meetings which have been well attended during the Winter. The Trustees have thoroughly repaired the Chapel and the other trust property which has cost them more than 90£. Mr Cliff then kindly gave up one whole quarters claim on the Rents & Mr Haward & Mr Moore and some other friends have subscribed towards it. But there is still nearly 60£ owing…

Cliff himself tried in July to help matters by inviting Browne to a Walpole 'tea and public meeting'. He clearly wanted to discuss the future with him. There is no record of Browne attending and we must assume that he did not attend as the Walpole deacons, possibly guided by Harvey and Cliff, decided to go ahead with a plan which a few weeks later was to provide the chaotic climax to this whole affair.

~

1871 During July, John Browne unexpectedly received from a Halesworth nonconformist two anonymous letters. Fortunately, he did not destroy them but filed them away with his official correspondence. They were written (in capitals) several weeks apart but overlap in content. What follows is an amalgam of the two.

> *Halesworth, 11/25 July*
> I hope you will excuse the liberty I take, but knowing you are a minister of influence in the county union I thought you might use that influence in trying to get the old Independents back to the Chapel again. Although not an Independent myself I do feel a great interest in both parties and should rejoice to see them all as one again. Nor do I think the Gracious Master would be grieved with such a proceeding. I do think there ought to be rules in the county union that if a church disagree it should be settled by arbitration. Now I do know when it was offered at Halesworth Mr Harvey's party consented but the Baptists at the Independent Chapel said they would not arbitrate. They form a very large body and the leading men are Baptists.[41] I must say they ought not to govern an Independent Church. Some of these are so very high in doctrine that they won't hear a good Independent Minister. Mr Carey was here a fortnight ago and I know several of the Baptists who went to hear him in the morning would not go again because they did not like him. I went to hear him in the evening and liked him very much. I think if he were to preach a few Sundays the Baptists would all leave. Then the old Independents might go back again. I know there is one of the deacons, if not he acts as one, carrying about the bread and wine on an ordinance Sunday who has been a member of a strict Baptist church. Some of those narrow-minded ones made quite a derision of good Mr Carey. I know it's true because I reproved several of them for doing it. I have been a few times to hear Mr Cliff. He is a very excellent young man and promises to be a fine preacher, is deserving a good church and draws many people to hear him. I hope you will do what you can…
>
> *Not An Independent But One Who Loves To See Unity In Churches.*

These were very likely views which produced an echo among many of the Quay Street congregation. But, throughout this affair, moderate views seem to have had little effect upon the conduct of the church. One has to

41 I cannot wholly explain why Baptists dominated this Congregational church as they seem to have done. The records of the Halesworth Baptists (SRO(L)353) show no defections to the Independents, but I believe it was not Baptist practice to record such happenings. They were Particular Baptists, in whose ranks there had recently been dissension about Open Communion – the administration of the Lord's Supper to those who had not been baptised by immersion. It is probable that the Quay Street Congregationalists practised a liberal policy as regards those eligible to take Communion and therefore had originally provided a religious home for the wandering Baptists. The Quay Street liberality, however, does not seem to have attracted the same spirit in return. See E. Payne, *The Baptist Union,* 1958, pp 87-90.

ask if there was not something seriously wrong with the government of a church in which a few obstinate figures at the top could obstruct what was, to all reasonable argument, the way to peace and order.[42]

1871

For four years Browne, Flower and Carey had been trying unsuccessfully to persuade the leaders of the senior Halesworth Church to accept arbitration – the anonymous letter-writer was by no means alone in urging this course. In, September they drafted a proposal to be put to the Suffolk Congregational Union. It was to add the following clause to the constitution:

> That the churches associated with the Union agree to submit to its arbitration any differences which may arise amongst them of so serious a character as to threaten disruption or secession. The decision of four fifths of the arbitrators appointed at one annual general meeting, when confirmed by the next such meeting, shall be final and any church refusing to submit to such decision shall *ipso facto* cease to be associated with the Union.[43]

In Quay Street the proposition was rejected outright:

> *Halesworth Minute Book, 15 September*
> It was resolved upon the motion of Mr Ives, seconded by Mr Haward, that the resolution to be proposed at the next Annual Conference of the Suffolk C. U. relating to the settlement of differences in our churches is in our opinion subversive of the great principle of Church Government as recognised by the whole body of Congregational Churches. We cannot therefore sanction or be bound by such resolution.

Enough material there for a renewed storm, but not as angry as the one which was about to break. At the offices of the *Halesworth Times* in Market Square the type was already being set for an apparently innocent advertisement announcing, at long last, Pastor Cliff's Ordination at Walpole. As can be seen overleaf it went rather further than that. It also sought to legitimise the New Congregational Church at Haleworth, which was precisely what the Suffolk Union had forbidden. Whether Cliff and Harvey were being devious or not, Seaman at Walpole was nothing but an innocent dupe. He is very unlikely to have composed the 'bill' and he certainly did not deserve the broadside he received from Flower:

> *Flower to Seaman, 17 September*
> I was surprised at receiving on Saturday a bill [poster] announcing services in connection with the Ordn. of Mr Cliff. You will remember that a Comm. was appointed by the County Union to arrange what was most prudent to be done in the matter of Walpole Church & the Halesworth

42 See MINISTERS under Some Definitions on page 9.

43 This text, handwritten by Browne on the printed *Rules of the Union*, is among the pages of the Halesworth Church Minute Book in the Suffolk Record Office at Lowestoft. His proposal proved not to be popular with other churches and was eventually dropped.

ORDINATION SERVICES
AND
HARVEST TEA MEETING.

The Ordination and Recognition of the

REV. R. A. CLIFF,

AS PASTOR of the

NEW CONGREGATIONAL CHURCH,
HALESWORTH,

AND OF THE

INDEPENDENT CHURCH, WALPOLE,

WILL TAKE PLACE

ON FRIDAY, SEPTEMBER THE 22ND, 1871.

The Ordination Services will be commenced at WALPOLE CHAPEL at half-past Two o'clock.

After the Scripture Lessons, and Prayer by the Rev. J. C. SALISBURY, of Cratfield, an Address will be delivered by the Rev. C. S. CAREY, of Bungay, on "*Independency:---The Churches of Christ independent of the State and of one another.*

The USUAL QUESTIONS will be asked by the REV. J. M. UFFEN, of Sawston, Cambridgeshire, and the ORDINATION PRAYER offered by the REV. P. COLBORNE, of Norwich.

The CHARGE TO THE MINISTER will be given by the Rev. T. TUFFIELD, of Woolwich.

A PUBLIC TEA

WILL BE HELD IN THE

ASSEMBLY ROOM, HALESWORTH,

At half-past Five. After which,

A PUBLIC MEETING

In connection with the Ordination Service, and also in commemoration of the Harvest.

EDWARD GRIMWADE, ESQ., OF IPSWICH IN THE CHAIR.

The following Addresses will be given:---*To the two Churches,* by the REV. S. BASDEN, of Denton; "*On the Duties of Sister Churches,*" by the Rev. J. M. UFFEN; "*The Extension of the Redeemer's Kingdom by Nonconformist Churches,*" by the Rev. P. COLBORNE. Subjects in connection with the Harvest will be treated by the Rev. D. Jones, of Brandeston; Rev. E. W. Wilson, of Southwold; and W. Jameson, Esq., of London.

TICKETS FOR THE TEA, NINEPENCE EACH,

(Children under Twelve, 6d. each,) may be had of Messrs. White, Roe, Smith, Hadingham, Gostling and Fyfe, Haleswoth, and Seaman, Walpole.

Historic Chapels Trust

The 'Bill' that caused the trouble …

secession. The Committee thought it desirable if possible to effect a union between them. We secured the retirement of Mr Haas that this might be done. We supposed that all further steps would be taken at least with our concurrence & sanction & that nothing would be done in the matter without our knowledge and advice.

1871

Instead of this we found that Mr Cliff had received an invitation to become the pastor of the Ch at Walpole, no stipulation having been made that the Halesworth secession should be incorporated with you or united to you. The consequence is that Mr Cliff is now pastor of two separate independent churches, which is a new thing in our denomination and altogether unconstitutional.

Time passes & there is not an opportunity for me to summon the Committee to meet before Friday – at least I fear not. I therefore as one member of tht Commee. write to you to protest against the arrangement which has been made & further to protest agnst. the manner in wh the Commee. has been treated in the matter & to declare that an Ordn. under such circumst'ces must meet with the condemnation of the Union & of all who are interested in the character & prosperity of our denomination.

I am very sorry to be obliged to write but I think you have been overreached and overpersuaded & I hope you will see that this is the case & that you will withhold your concurrence in the Ordination & so far at least as Walpole is concerned will quash the proceedings.

PS: the bill is in all its parts a studied insult to the Union & ostentatiously sets at naught all its recommendations.

Other outraged letters were being written, many on the same day therefore crossing in the post and adding to the general confusion.

Grimwade to Browne, 17 September

The "Bill" came to me yesterday & upon its receipt my soul was filled with indignation & I wrote by last night's post to Harvey, to whom I gave promise to attend, that it was a fraud. He had asked me to attend the Ordination of Mr Cliff over the Church at Walpole & Halesworth & that I could not sanction such a breach of contract. I wrote also to Mr Carey & said "We are sold" & begd. him to prevent his brethren attending & not go himself. Pray stop Wilson.[44] I will write Basden[45] tonight. I endorse all you say. Let me hear by return. Cant you summon a Committee Meeting for Tuesday or see Messrs Flower & Carey tomorrow who…should issue a protest & confer with the Trustees of Walpole to stop. It is possible but I fear it too late: but I say let's.

Carey to Browne 17 September

My dear Brother, I have withdrawn my engagement at Walpole and I think Grimwade will do the same. I will send your letter to Colborne.[46]

44 Rev. E.W. Wilson, Minister at Southwold from 1865.

45 Rev. F.S. Basden, Minister at Denton, Norfolk, from 1851.

46 Rev. Philip Colborne, (1831-1900), first minister of the Chapel-in-the-Field, Norwich, 1859-1884; Secretary of the Norfolk Congregational Union; afterwards at Lozells Chapel, Birmingham.

Rev. P. Colborne, to Browne, Norwich, 17 September

1871

Your letter on the ordination business requires haste so I write to say that I fear I have fallen unwittingly into a mistake about this whole Halesworth business – in this way. On my return from a rather long journey I found a letter waiting begging me to take part in these services. I could not reply till Monday September 4th. Before doing so, as I have not liked all I have heard of this Halesworth movement, I asked two friends who know Suffolk about it. One told me she thought peace was restored between the parties at Halesworth, another that a Committee of your union had been working at the matter. Now connecting this with the letter to attend "ordination of Mr Cliff as Pastor of the Walpole & Halesworth churches" and seeing that Carey & Grimwade both active members as I supposed of your Union had already consented to attend I came, too hastily I fear, to the conclusion that reconciliation not strife & division were to characterise these meetings. Still I wrote cautiously saying that as no definite break had been presented to me I must decline being present. By rail came another immediately upon receipt of mine saying they wanted me to offer the ordination prayer & speak upon the subject against which my name stands in the bill and begging for an immediate reply. I certainly felt attracted to both these pieces of work and hoping all was right consented.

I am afraid however as I look at the Bill that your view of the case is the right one and that two little separate churches not two churches united are to have one pastor to divide between them. I am probably more opposed even than you are to this sort of thing, having spent as much time and energy as I could in amalgamating and affiliating little once separate churches in this county.

Of course I cannot go to the Meeting if such is their character & enclose copy of a letter which I send to Halesworth this post which I shall thank you to consider private & confidential till you have heard further from me.

In conclusion let me say there was one feeling prompting me to consent to this application which is still strong upon me – that is to join with Suffolk brethren in their work & union – it is not that I want work but think the County Unions should have more fellowship. All the years I have been at Norwich I have only once been asked to do anything in connection with your Union. This is not personal or I should not mention it. It is the wish of Hallett[47] & Barrett[48] I believe. Our Union may be as much in fault – "2 blacks do not make a white" – and you in Suffolk are larger and stronger & do more work than we can to have wider opportunites for fellowship.

Colborne to Seaman, 17 September

I fear from looking carefully at your bill that "The ordination and recognition of the Rev R.A. Cliff as pastor of the new Congregational Church,

47 Rev. John Hallett, Minister at the Norwich Old Meeting, 1856-1880.

48 Rev. G.S. Barrett, Minister at Prince's Street Chapel, Norwich, 1866-1910. A noted hymnologist, he was to edit the Congregational Church Hymnal of 1887.

Halesworth, and of the Independent church Walpole" clearly means that these two religious communities are – and are intended to be – separate and distinct & that the intention is to recognise Mr Cliff as pastor of two separate churches. What I perhaps too hastily inferred from your note inviting me to "the ordination of Mr Cliff as Pastor of the Walpole & Halesworth churches" was that these churches were united; & as such amalgamation of small separate churches has been one of the objects dear to my heart, for which in this county I have steadily laboured & do still labour, I was inclined to be with you at such a desirable celebration.

1871

If however I am mistaken here, I have mistaken altogether the character of your meeting & certainly can take no part in it whatever. It would be a solemn mockery on my part to ask God to bless what my convictions lead me to think He does not approve – the multiplication of little separate churches.

Should my first impression be the right one that you have already amalgamated Walpole & Halesworth or affiliated one to the other so that they now exist as the united church of Walpole & Halesworth I will gladly come but if not I must hold my self quite disengaged from the whole matter into which I am sorry tht I did not make further inquiry though pressed as I was.

Rev. F.S. Basden to Browne, 18 September

I am not accustomed to act against my Brethren, but it was not for me to object to the wording of the "Bill" as I have taken no part in your County Union affairs – but, finding that the names which were a guarantee that all things would be done decently & in order are withdrawn I at once wrote to Halesworth to withdraw.

Browne was writing and travelling all over the area to forestall the ordination. On 18 September he said to John Flower: 'I think our Halesworth friends have now completely overreached themselves and have got themselves in a pretty fix'. The following day Robert Haward of Walpole writes to confess that he is just as surprised as anybody:

Robert Haward to Browne, 19 September

I have received an invitation to attend the meetings at Walpole and Halesworth and replied that I would go to Walpole but no further. I am anxious that poor old Walpole shall be settled, and having seen the names of Messrs. Grimwade, Carey, Jones and Wilson all members of the Union on the Bill, supposed the proceedings next Friday were about to be taken with the sanction of the Union. But as Mr Cliff has been elected to the Walpole pastorate I do not see how you can prevent his ordination over that church with its 10 (more or less) members. I am sorry you wrote Mr Seaman.[49] He is a journeyman carpenter, a weak man, and led by Cliff anywhere. His wife who plays the harmonium at Walpole, has a most sad reputation, and is the woman about whom so much was said in connection

49 The text of this letter is lost.

with Haas. Please write per return and if you tell me Messrs Grimwade, Carey & Colborne have not consented to their names appearing in the posting bills I will not go to Walpole. Who is Mr J. Uffen of Sawston, Cambridgeshire? Mr W. Moore of Peasenhall is the old deacon of the Walpole church, one of the trustees, and a good man. You may rely upon him.

1871

The flurry of letters did its job. A second poster was hastily printed and although meetings and teas took place, the ordination of Richard Athol Cliff did not.

Robert Haward writes again to Browne almost immediately, revealing some of the shadier side of what had been going on. It is not quite the Haward we have known – gentle and a little above the battle:

Robert Haward to Browne, 23 September

The result of the letters they received was the issuing of a second poster stating that owing to the serious illness of the "officiating minister" Mr Tuffield,[50] and other circumstances, which will be explained, the ordination is unavoidably postponed but a sermon will be preached in Walpole Chapel by Rev. J. M. Uffen in the afternoon, and a tea meeting in the Assembly Room, Halesworth, in the evening. And I suppose these meetings took place yesterday. And now we shall hear of the persecution to which these "lambs" are subjected. And ultimately the Wesleyans will take them in hand. I find they are coquetting with the church party in Halesworth and that Mr Cliff took tea with the rector a fortnight since. On Thursday one of their body called me in and was very full of denunciation of the oppressive tyranny to which they were exposed. I asked who was the tyrant and he said "Browne of Wrentham" had been writing letters to the ministers and one to Mr Seaman, which he had seen, asking him to put a stop to the meeting at Walpole. You will probably soon hear more of this.

And he did. Browne had his informants everywhere, even in Quay Street.

Samuel Brown [deacon at Quay Street] *to Browne, 23 September*

Mr Wilson (of Southwold) was at both services and promised to come immediate with all respecting the day – I will therefore only say in general. The Two Services were well attended – Explanation in the Afternoon only, "The County Secy's influence with the Ministers, the Cause" – not much said about it, a few side wind remarks in the evening – I will watch the Local Papers and forward as requested – Tuffield, the Presiding M. ill, Rheumatic Fever – am sorry I cannot be at Wrentham till the 15th.

Rev. E.W. Wilson to Browne, Southwold, 24 September

There was no letter or notice from Halesworth on Thursday but yesterday morning I read a "Bill" announcing that the Ordination wd. be unavoidably postponed on account of the serious illness of the presiding minister and

50 Rev. Thomas Tuffield (1823-1883). Congregational minister, with a Wesleyan background, at Woolwich since 1850. 2000 mourners attended his funeral. He was most likely a mentor of Cliff's.

THE
ORDINATION SERVICE
WHICH WAS ADVERTISED TO TAKE PLACE AT
WALPOLE,
IS
UNAVOIDABLY POSTPONED
On account of the Serious Illness of the PRESIDING MINISTER, and other adverse circumstances which will be fully explained. But
A SERMON
WILL BE PREACHED IN WALPOLE CHAPEL, BY THE
REV. J. MC. CLUNE UFFEN,
Of SAWSTON. Service commencing at half-past Two.

THE HARVEST
TEA MEETING
WILL BE HELD, (AS ANNOUNCED) IN THE
ASSEMBLY ROOM, HALESWORTH,
On FRIDAY NEXT, SEPTEMBER 22nd, 1871,
Tea at half-past Five o'clock.
TICKETS, NINEPENCE EACH.
(Children under Twelve years of age 6d. each); may be had of Messrs. White, Roe, Smith, Hadingham, Gostling, and Fyfe, Halesworth; and Seaman, Walpole.

S. B. FYFE, PRINTER, HALESWORTH.

Historic Chapels Trust

… and the one which tried to put things right. Both hang in Walpole Old Chapel.

other adverse circs. wh. wd. be fully explnd., & that a sermon wd. be preached in aftern. by Uffen, the harvest meeting being as announced. About 25 of us went. The explanation was that the Ordination was postponed on accnt. of all of the ministers who had promised to take part withdrawing from the Engagement through the representations (or some such word) of the Cnty. Secy. I heard by the way that Tuffield was very ill with rheumatic fever, otherwise the ordination wd. have been proceeded with.

1871

The evening meeting was a glorious one. They resolved beforehand to say nothing about the Ordination – nor did they – except that Cliff sd. he had felt almost crushed during the week. Basden was there & gave a good harvest address. I shd. say there were about 500 people present. Several Wesleyan brethren spoke. Though they bottled up their wrath last night I expect they will give it vent when they report the meetings. I cd. not help feeling as I sat there that a minister and people who could lay hold of the populace as they seem to have done, have a claim to both recognition and sympathy. They have proved their right to exist by their zeal & success. It is a pity the whole thing cannot be solved in a way satisfactory to both parties.

The *Halesworth Times* reporter had more of an eye for the romance of the Harvest Tea than the key facts. He noted the exquisite floral decoration of the Halesworth Assembly Room, 'resembling more the dwelling place of fairy sprites than the mart where farmer and merchant, buyer and seller were weekly wont to drive hard bargains'. He noted that Mr Newman, landlord of the Angel Inn, had lent a pony and trap to bring in shrubs and evergreens from the villages around. He noted the 'fervency and fire' of the many speakers, but not what any of them said. Only then did he note the significant fact that the disappointed members of the 'Free' Congregational Church were supported by sympathisers from the Established church and the Wesleyans.

The reporter of the *Suffolk Chronicle* had a little more sinew to him. He reported verbatim the attack made on Browne at the afternoon service in Walpole Chapel by the Rev. J. McClune Uffen[51] of Sawston, Cambridgeshire:

Suffolk Chronicle, 26 September
"... It is necessary to explain the position which I occupy this afternoon. Most of you are present to witness, and I originally came to take part in, the Ordination of the Rev. R.A. Cliff. In obedience, however, to the behest of the Secretary of the Suffolk Congregational Union, the ministers (with the exception of the Rev. T. Tuffield, of Woolwich, who I regret to say is dangerously ill) whose names have been announced have withdrawn

51 Rev. J. McLune Uffen (1845-1923), Minister, Sawston, Cambridgeshire; Queen's Walk, Nottingham; Dorchester for 21 years. 'Many young men entered the ministry through his influence' said the *Congregational Year Book* at his death.

from their engagement. I am here not withstanding for two reasons. First, the Secretary of the Suffolk Union has not written a line to me, and therefore I am directly unaware of any local objection to the proposed service. Secondly, the gentlemen whose names are upon the bill, with one exception, have individually recognised the new church and minister at Halesworth: they have either preached to the people or have been present at their meetings and Mr Cliff has been invited to their pulpits and platforms in return. I am surprised, and doubtless you will be too, that all this has been done without any intimation being sent to Mr Cliff himself."

1871

My dear Friend
The "Bill" came to me
Yesterday & upon the receipt
my soul was filled with
indignation & I wrote
by last night post to Harvey
to whom I gave promise
to attend that it was a
fraud. He had ask'd me
to attend the Ordination of

Official indignation expressed by Grimwade and Browne

Yours very truly
John Browne

I think our Halesworth friends have now
completely overreached themselves & have got
themselves into a pretty fix.

5
AFTERMATH
1871–1874

It is to the newspapers that John Browne now turns, fighting his battle in public. The bitterness of it all is now out. In the *Halesworth Times* he writes a letter of a thousand words defending himself and justifying the Suffolk Union for its part in the fiasco. He launches a personal attack on Cliff, now a very popular figure in the town,[52] designed to play upon the strongest of Suffolk prejudices.

Halesworth Times, 3 October

> ...A total stranger to the neighbourhood came from a distance, and having only an ex-parte knowledge of the facts of the case, presided at the formation of the [seceding] church and so commenced the series of mistakes which has ended in the collapse of the plans for the ordination on Friday last.

For the rest, his letter was a not-too-concise recital of the happenings of the previous 18 months. A week later, Joseph Harvey launched a counter-attack which was three times as long. The blast and counter-blast continued week-by-week for another two months.[53]

During this public campaign Browne took the opportunity of turning his increasingly scornful attack on the youthful minister who had preached the critical sermon in Walpole Chapel: the Rev. J. McLune Uffen. The core of Browne's objections to what had so nearly happened was that the joining of two 'causes', the running of two congregations under one minister, amounted to what he called 'spiritual adultery'. Not unnaturally, Uffen strongly objected to the term and he wrote, for publication in the newspaper, that an authority he had consulted in his own district (the Rev. W. Cuthbertson of Bishops Stortford[54]) had disagreed strongly with Browne's line, saying that such a union of two churches was 'neither unscriptural nor unconstitutional; and that contention is most childish and absurd'.

52 In Halesworth Cemetery, the gravestone of the 10-week-old son of Samuel Smith, carriage-maker and member of Richard Athol Cliff's breakaway church, shows that the child was named Ernest Athol. Undoubtedly a tribute to the young minister.

53 The *Halesworth Times* files are on microfilm at the Lowestoft and Ipswich branches of the SRO.

54 Rev. W. Cuthbertson (1827-1910), Spring Hill, Birmingham; Ebenezer, West Bromwich; Pitt Street, Sydney, NSW; Bishops Stortford 1863-1880; Chairman, Congregational Union of England and Wales 1879. A few weeks after these events he was in Swansea, seconding Dr Dale's motion attacking Gladstone's government for penalising nonconformists in the 1870 Education Act.

Browne's dismissal of Uffen went like this:

Halesworth Times, 13 November *1871*

...Lastly, I decline altogether to enter into a controversy with Mr Uffen, a young gentleman who has been three or four years connected with the Congregational body, and who in that time has learnt more than they ever knew who were studying and working Congregational principles before he was born – who thinks that he was the right person to be written to, and that he was shelved because he was likely to dispute my authority and to question my judgment – I say a young gentleman like this is evidently one with whom it would be only presumptuous folly in me to entertain. I have now done with this controversy...

John Browne was as good as his word. In the six further years that were to pass before the matter was settled he had little more to say about it in public.

But Uffen was a skilful, if bumptious, 26-year-old who, in years to come, was to build a substantial reputation for himself. Five years after these events he presented a much-applauded paper to the Cambridgeshire Congregational Union on the Supply of Ministers. The directness and vigour displayed there are present in this cheeky but effective reply to Browne:

Halesworth Times, 22 November

Sir,

In his letter of last week, Mr Browne declines to enter into any controversy with me; and as a stress is laid upon the fact of my youth, I judge that to be his reason...He forgets that the discussion was opened by himself, and that not in a very courteous fashion, and the final clause in his last production, far exceeds in contemptuous expression anything advanced by them.

"Mr Uffen is a young gentleman". I am not anxious to rebut the charge, but I strongly dispute his use of the fact to insult me. He will, perhaps, kindly consider that:

1. I am a young man. But that has not disqualified me from conducting the affairs of one of the largest and most flourishing churches in this county. I also sit on the Committee of the Union.[55] As a recognised minister of this denomination, whether old or young, I was entitled to a communication from him. It was my right both ecclesiastically, as well as socially and religiously.

2. I am a young man. And therefore, as I stated, obtained the opinion of two men who are authorities in the denomination, one of whom has been forty years in the ministry. It was their view that I advanced and which Mr Browne cannot meet. He may sneer at the man but he cannot parry the thrust.

55 Presumably the one in Cambridgeshire.

3. I am a young man. I am not for that however incompetent for church membership, nor ministerial office. But according to Mr Browne I am disqualified to pass a judgment upon ecclesiastical principles. I may act but must not think nor speak. Two and two make four, and three and three make six; but I must wait until I am older before I admit or declare the truth of these propositions.

1871

etc, etc,
Yours respectfully,
J. McLune Uffen

There was, among all these reciprocal insults between Uffen and Browne and Harvey, only one issue which was of any substance: the question of whether Browne was on firm ground when he claimed that it was improper for one minister to be pastor of two churches. Leave aside the Uffen view, there does appear to have been substantial opinion among senior Congregationalists that there was nothing terribly shocking in the idea. It would be understandable if Browne had been so exhausted by the battle that his judgment had become a little shaky.

After all those months of drama there was the inevitable lull for recuperation. It is hard to discern any particular pattern of activity. Cliff became the acknowledged pastor at Walpole, although there is no record of a formal ordination having taken place. Yet the records of the Suffolk Congregational Union do show him attending its conferences. The Walpole Church Book contains only one entry from his six years there – it shows that in 1874 the old chapel had no more than fourteen members.[56]

Browne and his colleagues on the Suffolk Union, still bruised by their treatment at the hands of self-assured young ministers who had infiltrated their territory and treated them with scant respect, tried to improve their defences against any recurrence. The following appears in the minute book of their Executive Committee:

Suffolk Union Minute Book, 19 December
Mr Flower moved, and Mr H. Read seconded, & it was carried unanimously, that it is desirable to recommend to the Annual Meeting that a standing sub-committee be appointed, or that it shall be an instruction to the Executive

56 The Walpole members in 1874 are listed as Mr & Mrs Seaman, Mr & Mrs W. Moore, Mrs S. White, Mrs Wray of Chediston, Mrs Morse, Naomi Hurren, Mr & Mrs Forster of Cookley, Mrs Hamer (later removed to Stradbroke), Mr W. Hurren of Huntingfield, Mr & Mrs Crane. As ever, distinction must be drawn between 'members', the core of the church, and 'hearers' who may have attended particular services. The Church Book itself covers the years from 1809 to 1970 when the congregation formally ceased to exist. It was discovered a few years ago walled up in the Halesworth shop premises of a former trustee, Mr E.E. Roe. It is being added to the Walpole archive material already held by the Suffolk Record Office at Ipswich.

> Committee for the time being, to investigate the character and standing of every new minister of the denomination coming into this County.

1871-3

They did not say what criteria they intended to use. The young Cliff was certainly an unknown, and perhaps a threatening, force. But, much later, at King's Lynn and nearby Hunstanton he seems to have built a remarkable reputation. In 1918 the Norfolk Congregational Union presented him with an address bearing testimony that during 50 years he had 'supported every movement for the welfare of the people'. The benign countenance of his mature photograph (page 29) conceals what had clearly been a radical instinct. Perhaps that is what frightened John Browne.

The Quay Street Church's register of members shows that a small number of those who seceded in 1867 were, at this time, accepted back by the 'old' church. Within that church the old divisions remained. There is no firm evidence on which to judge the activities and standing of the Minister, Abraham Jackson. James Newby (page 23, note 3) was perhaps too close to the families involved, and he himself later being a deacon of the church, to be a totally revealing historian of its past.

By 1873 the power struggle began to emerge once again. There had been a fresh initiative from the Suffolk Union urging the two parties to submit their differences to arbitration. As so often before, the New Church was accepting while a majority of deacons at the Old Church were persuaded to stick to their guns.

But now Samuel Brown, the Quay Street grocer, began to move strongly towards a negotiated settlement. He went as far as unilaterally calling a meeting of the deacons to discuss a softer approach. The steely John Bedwell was so outraged at the idea of moderation that he questioned Samuel Brown's propriety in even thinking of it:

> *Halesworth Minute Book, 8 July 1873*
> *Mr Bedwell raised the following question*: the propriety or right of any individual member of the Committee to call a meeting. After some discussion Mr Bedwell etc moved that in future – in the case of special meetings – no individual member be permitted to do so without consulting the body. Mr Brown explained his motive in calling the meeting together and submitted the papers attached hereto for discussion on the subject of reunion stating that great obstacles were now removed and that we might enter upon the subject with hopeful expectation of success. After some little discussion, which was neither pleasant nor profitable, Mr Bedwell moved that there was not sufficient ground (in the paper submitted by Mr Brown). *2nd by G. Haward, & carried with two dissentients.*

The minute book of 22 July records that the meeting voted to erase the words 'neither pleasant nor profitable' from the record. But they are still there for us to glimpse what sort of battle had taken place. Bedwell then struck a further tactical blow at Brown.

1873-4

Proposed by Mr Bedwell: that the paper read by Mr Brown at the last cttee meeting be not entered on our minutes but returned to him – *carried*.

This was too much for Brown and eventually he resigned from the deacons' committee. On the day following, Bedwell did so as well.

Samuel Brown to Secretary, Halesworth Independent Church, 19 January
Dear Brethren, I regret under existing circumstances I cannot attend in Committee as at present constituted.

John Bedwell to Committee, Halesworth Independent Church, 20 January
Dear Brethren, I have for these last six months contemplated the step I am now determined to take. I am fully convinced the overbearing spirit I have witnessed precludes the possibility of our working on harmoniously. Besides, I consider the meetings of the Committee as so much waste time, if one person presumes to disregard the decision of the Majority. Therefore I decline serving on the Committee for the ensuing year.[57]

57 These two letters are pasted into the Halesworth Minute Book.

Halesworth.
Jany 20. 1874.

To the Committee of the
Congregational Church.

Dear Brethren,

I have for these last six Months contemplated the step I am now determined to take. I am fully convinced the overbearing Spirit I have witnessed precludes the possibility of our working on harmoniously, besides I consider the meetings of the Committee as so much waste time, if one person presumes to disregard the decision of the Majority. therefore I decline Serving on the Committee for the ensuing Year.

Wishing you all needful wisdom
I am Yours faithfully
John Bedwell.

SRO, Ipswich

The tax collector versus the grocer.

David Holmes

Gravestones of the Haward family at the Congregational Chapel, Bramfield. The Charles Haward mentioned is one of the three brothers central to 'The Affair'. Robert Haward in the foreground was their father. His son Robert, acting Trustee at Walpole, lies beyond, just out of sight.

7

ARMISTICE
1876–1877

The Quay Street deacons were stuck on a sandbank waiting to be rescued. Indeed, they appear not to have met again until the end of 1876. Details of the intervening years can only be found from the Church Book. The storms raging between the opposing wings of the church continued. But then a patch of blue sky appeared and rescue seemed to be at hand:

> *Halesworth Minute Book, 26 March, 1876*
> Mr Charles Haward having expressed a desire to re-unite with this Church was unanimously received, and welcomed by the Pastor.

Charles Haward, aged 61, the middle of the three Haward brothers, had been a member at Quay Street in his youth, but had left to join the Baptists. It is possible that he had become a member of Harvey's New Congregational Church, but there is no recorded proof. He owned Holly Farm in Bramfield, alongside the land of his two brothers, Robert and George. He was a lay preacher, a total abstainer, and an enthusiast for deep cultivation of the soil, especially by means of a steam cultivator which he owned and let out for hire. Where George was combative and unyielding, Charles had a reputation for calm wisdom. Whether his return to Quay Street was a matter of personal decision or part of a planned move towards re-unification, it could not have been more beneficial. The healing process began almost immediately.

In August, George Haward and his wife decided to move 'to a distant part of the country', which turned out to be Hastings in Sussex. He resigned as Secretary of the Church and departed soon after. He had been Secretary for 26 years. He was succeeded by Charles's nephew Robert Ebenezer Haward who remained in that position until 1923.[58]

Then on 11 February 1877 the Pastor, Abraham Jackson, announced to a Church Meeting that he was to become minister at Debenham, a sizeable Suffolk village 15 miles to the west. He resigned with these words:

58 Another prominent local man who is thought to have been influential in bringing the two sides together was Benjamin Roe. He became a member of the Quay Street church in 1859 but shortly afterwards, still a young man, moved to London. Returning in the mid-70s, Roe joined the Assembly Room church until the reunion of 1877. He became a deacon and later treasurer and Superintendant of the Sunday School. Roe ran a highly successful grocery and drapery business in Market Place.

> It is with much pain I am constrained to sever our union as Pastor and People; but the Divine Master, whose I am and whom I serve, has intimated his will, I believe most clearly and unmistakably, that I should labour in another part of the Vineyard.

1877

He knew that nothing could be mended unless he, and Cliff also, moved on to other parts. Cliff went 10 miles off to Harleston, just over the Norfolk border.

Almost immediately after these departures had taken place the mood changed. Friendly exchanges went on in private until Charles Haward, fortified by what he called 'a joyous increase of loving', one day put this crucial proposition to the Church Meeting:

> *Halesworth Church Book, 25 March*
> We as members composing the Church of Christ worshipping at Quay Street Meeting House, Halesworth, do hereby earnestly and cordially invite all and everyone of our brethren and sisters composing the Church of Christ worshipping in the Assembly Room in this town, henceforth with us to unite, each severally, to form one Church upon the broad basis of our common faith. That a copy of this resolution be forwarded to the other church…

The letter was sent and Harvey replied promptly. But this man who experienced unqualified anger all too easily could not bear the thought of unqualified joy. He accepted the invitation and the greetings, but was ready with his 'ifs' and 'buts':

> *Letter from Harvey dated 27 March in Halesworth Church Book*
> In order to secure the continuing peace and harmony of the Church thus united we think it desirable, and we have reason to think you will concur in this, namely that a minute should be entered in the Book seeking to rectify the record of events of 1867 and fully to clear and vindicate the Christian character and reputation of all the members of the Church at that date. And we would suggest for this purpose…that this re-union will render necessary that a small committee be appointed of persons, in equal numbers, from both churches. This being done we shall be prepared cordially and affectionately to accept your invitation…

Charles Haward, peacemaker though he might be, was having none of that. The record shows him firmly putting the senior church's view:

> *Halesworth Church Book, 2 April*
> 1. That the simultaneous action of the two Churches, both in future co-operation and unity, must be on the basis alone of unconditional union and not re-union. 2. Any references to the records of either Church whether by discussion or minute must be absolutely avoided. 3. That the appointment of a joint committee of the two Churches could only be for arrangement of details and not for consideration of principles of action.

Sharp words, however loving, may well have been exchanged, because Harvey immediately withdrew:

1877

Harvey to Charles Haward, 4 April

Having duly considered this important subject we do hereby cordially and affectionately accept, wishing that the Holy Spirit of God bring increased spirituality and growth in grace to each and all of us.

The doors were now fully open and 43 members of the breakaway church were to re-enter through them. Where grudging compliments and stony conservatism had been spoken, generosity and gratitude now poured out from Quay Street. Emotion, other than that of anger, had not been a feature of this affair. But it is hard not to be moved by the intensity of the reaction which now showed itself at the thought of old friends being able to combine in their worship once again:

Halesworth Church Book, 15 April

Charles Haward proposed and Samuel Brown seconded: that this Church having received from the Sister Church meeting at the Assembly Room a warm, cordial and unanimous acceptance of our Invitation to unite with us in fellowship as one Church, desires to express the joyous anticipations we cherish in respect of such nearly realized union and also the fervent desire we entertain to welcome to the sanctuary all who have been fellow-worshippers with the Sister Church.

That all sittings be open and free for Lord's Day, April 29, and the two following Sabbaths, and that with a view to general convenience and re-arrangement of the pews the cards at present appended to the pews and sittings shall be removed after next Lord's Day the 22nd instant...the united church, meeting in this Vestry at the usual time, will at once proceed to appoint officers...such officers being nominated by the joint Committee of the two churches...

Minutes of the first meeting of the United Church, 29 April

It was a unanimous recommendation that four Members should be at once appointed Deacons of the Church...It was carried unanimously that Messrs. Samuel Brown, Joseph Harvey, Charles Haward and Benjamin Roe be appointed to sustain the office of Deacon amongst us.

These were the four people who had done most to bring the two churches back into union. And they had achieved it without the presence of a minister.[59]

In September 1877 a letter from John Browne was read to a special meeting of the Halesworth Church. He had two suggestions to make. One was to invite the whole Suffolk Congregational Union to meet in

59 It was not until the following April that the Rev. A.A. Dowsett came from Ridgewell in Essex. He was the first Congregational minister in Halesworth to be provided with a house and a guaranteed income – £150 a year.

Halesworth to celebrate the settlement. The other was to bring to heel the proud but nonetheless ramshackle old church at Walpole. It would live on for another 100 years or so, but with its independence blunted:

1877

Browne to Halesworth Church Meeting, 23 September

Whereas the old Congregational Church at Walpole is decayed and become so feeble as not to be able to maintain the public worship of God in its ancient sanctuary, it is therefore expedient that some means should be devised for continuing that worship...Upon the whole it has appeared that the most feasible plan is that the two Churches of Walpole and Halesworth should become Associated Churches for the more efficient working of Walpole under the present circumstances of depression. Notwithstanding that if, in the providence of God, there should arise a fair probability that the said Walpole Church could maintain its own independent existence, in that case the connection should cease and the Churches should resume their original independence if desired.

Only a fortnight later on 7 October the Halesworth Church agreed. The deal was done. A sort of peace had been established. But at a cost to the quaint, the truly radical, the independent. In religion as in the rest of life, the weak and inarticulate must surrender to the strong. The margin between understanding and misunderstanding would always be slight; and the frailty of human kind, however spiritually supported, would see to it that clashes continued to occur between individuals, their beliefs and their prejudices.

For the moment, the simple peace of compromise descended on this little arena in rural Suffolk. The terms of that compromise were barely mentioned. The singing of the *Gloria* seemed no longer an issue. What mattered most was that they had become one church again. Nor did they seem to have the least awareness that in the big world beyond, a hundred miles off at their Autumn Meeting in Leicester, more celebrated Congregationalists were arguing the issue which had so bedevilled the lives of these good Halesworth people for so many years: whether a spiritual body could survive if its members disagreed about the exact nature of its beliefs.

POSTSCRIPT

JOSEPH HARVEY AND THE *GLORIA*

One of the difficulties in joining up the bits of this book has been the complete absence of any direct evidence as to why Joseph Harvey, deacon and organist of the Quay Street Church, Halesworth, came in the first place to be asking the choir and congregation to sing the *Gloria*. There is no clue in the Church Book or the Deacons' minutes; nor, despite it being the *casus belli*, is it mentioned in more than one of the letters. Understandably, 136 years later, no hymn book or psalm or chant book of the time remains in the organ loft or vestry at Halesworth.

Did Harvey have connections within Congregationalism but outside his immediate domain who might have influenced him? A chance observation in Halesworth cemetery opened up a possibility. In the shadows of the nonconformist section stands a gravestone recording that on 11 November 1864 Caroline Mary Theodorick, 'eldest and much beloved child of Joseph and Caroline Harvey, died aged 15'. This was Harvey's daughter. She died not in Halesworth but in the village of Plaistow, standing on the Thames marshes, five miles downstream from the City of London – then in the county of Essex but now part of the thoroughly urban London borough of Newham.

The death certificate of Mary Harvey (as she was known) in the Newham registrar's files, records her as having died of 'typhus' while staying at an address on Broadway, Plaistow. How did this teenage daughter of a religious Halesworth schoolmaster happen to be there, 80 miles away, in November 1864? Kelly's Essex Directory of 1866 shows that in one of the few houses on Broadway the Misses Smith ran a 'seminary'. Was she a boarder there? If so, why there? Had some friend recommended the school to her father?

Just round the corner from Broadway was Richmond House, residence at the time of the educational pioneer John Curwen, for the past 22 years Congregational Minister at Plaistow. He was about to retire and give all his time to publishing books about *Tonic Sol-fa*, the system of musical notation he had developed. It was based on the work of Sarah Glover, a Norwich schoolmistress. From 1858 onwards Curwen produced a long series of books and articles on the use of *Sol-fa* in training congregations and Sunday school children to sing hymns, chants and anthems. All his chants had the *Gloria* attached.

Curwen's work was attracting growing attention in Britain and overseas. He spoke frequently and persuasively to nonconformist conferences.

He published many articles in the religious press. So it would be no surprise if he seized the interest of a Suffolk school-teacher and chapel organist wrestling with the training of a small choir among people unused to conventional musical notation. Might, indeed, their two families have become friendly? Curwen's papers are at present not available to researchers so I have not been able to establish the fact of any link. Nor has the Gooches' tireless work on the Harveys[60] yielded anything on this aspect.

~

The middle years of the 19th century were for Congregationalism a time of 'perplexity' and enormous change.[61] The foundations of Calvinism were under attack. In 1862 the noted London minister Henry Allon of the Union Chapel, Islington, had used these words to criticise the effect of Calvinism on Congregational worship:

> Calvin was utterly destitute of musical sensibility, as every page of his works and every element of his character indicate. He was too much of a theological formula to have much of the genius of song. And this unhappy defect has so deprived his writings of the broad human sympathy which so characterises Luther's, and has entailed upon all the churches that bear his name such musical asceticism and poverty...The unmusical Calvin has so impoverished Puritan and Presbyterian worship that its rugged, inartistic, slovenly psalmody has become a by-word and a needless repulsion. For surely there is no piety in discords, nor any special devoutness in slovenliness. Our nature craves something better than the traditional psalm-singing of the inharmonious meeting house. Our affinities are with whatever is best, whether in eloquence, poetry or music.[62]

An even more senior Congregationalist, the Rev. Thomas Binney,[63] had written complementary words a decade and more earlier. He pleaded for an approach to the reading of the Bible which bestowed on it 'a little more' expression:

> a flower or ornament now and then thrown in – something of a measured and musical cadence occasionally given to the diction, that it might be a pleasing and an appropriate vehicle for the history of song...

and he went on to urge that such an attitude might encourage the growth of singing in Congregational services:

> Psalmody is an essential part of public worship...in some churches it is the only exercise in which the people take part. They are vocal and active

60 For details of their book, see Sources, page 79.

61 R.Tudur Jones, *Congregationalism in England*. Chapter 6 offers a full account of these turbulent times.

62 Rev. H. Allon, (1818-1892), *Church Song and its Relations to Church Life*. Lecture to YMCA 1862.

63 Rev.Thomas Binney, (1798-1874), *The Service of Song in the House of the Lord*, 1848; from *Preface* and pp 40/41. Binney was Minister of the King's Weigh House Chapel, then in the City of London, from 1829-1869.

> only when they sing. Yet many of them habitually decline it. And this not from want of ability – for some of the silent sing well...the fault springs from want of thought, from inattention to, or ignorance of, the importance which God, in every age, has attached to praise; from a deficient sense of the duty itself, as duty; from a want of appreciation of the claims and dignity of worship as such; from a low state of the spiritual life; from extreme or mistaken views of external religion; or, in some worse cases, from spiritual pride...

Binney is credited with introducing the use of chants. Allon took his work further. Not only did he build a choir which could sing a wide range of religious music from many different traditions but he, with his organist the gifted Henry Gauntlett,[64] trained the congregation in the singing of psalms and anthems. Such were their new skills that they performed a section of the *Messiah* each Christmas Day.

But Allon and Gauntlett's most effective achievement was the publication of *The Congregational Psalmist* in 1862 which was so successful that it sold thousands of copies within a few years and went into many editions. It contained psalms and chants, each of them with the short *Gloria* appended. Such was the welcome given to it in the nonconformist press that there seems a reasonable chance that Joseph Harvey knew of it and had a copy.

That, however, would have put him at odds with the majority of members his church. In 1865 they had decided to buy the 'official' *New Congregational Hymn Book*, which contains no *Glorias*. It would be another 20 years before Congregational officialdom published a book[65] which was daring enough to take that step. Nonetheless, Allon's volume might have been a source of Harvey's interest in the *Gloria*.

64 Dr H.J. Gauntlett, (1805-1876), composer of *Once in Royal David's City* and thousands of other tunes and chants; Mendelssohn's choice as organist in the first performance of *Elijah* in Birmingham.

65 *The Congregational Church Hymnal* of 1887, edited by G.S. Barrett, minister at Prince's Street Chapel, Norwich.

WHO WAS WHO?

HALESWORTH INDEPENDENT CHURCH, QUAY STREET

BEDWELL, JOHN – deacon; tax collector; former Baptist
BROWN, SAMUEL – deacon; grocer, Quay Street
COLEMAN, REV. HENRY – minister 1864-1868
HAWARD, CHARLES – returned 1876; deacon; farmer
HAWARD, GEORGE – deacon; secretary 1850-76. Left for Hastings 1876
JACKSON, REV. ABRAHAM – minister 1869-1877

NEW CONGREGATIONAL CHURCH, ASSEMBLY ROOM

CLIFF, REV. RICHARD ATHOL – minister 1868-1877
HARVEY, JOSEPH BENJAMIN – deacon and secretary 1867-1877; headmaster, Castle Academy

WALPOLE CHAPEL

HAWARD, ROBERT – acting trustee; landowner, Bramfield
MOORE, WILLIAM – senior trustee; farmer, Peasenhall
SEAMAN, SIMON – deacon; journeyman carpenter, Walpole

SUFFOLK CONGREGATIONAL UNION

BROWNE, REV. JOHN – minister, Wrentham; secretary, East Suffolk CU
CAREY, REV. CHARLES STOKES – minister, Beccles until 1870; executive committee, SCU
FLOWER, REV. JOHN – minister, Bungay; executive committee, SCU
GRIMWADE, EDWARD – chairman; Mayor of Ipswich; tailor and outfitter
REEVE, REV. JONAH – minister, Stowmarket; executive committee, SCU

SOURCES

ANNUAL REGISTER, 1860-1880

BINFIELD, C., *Nonconformity in the Eastern Counties 1840-1885, with Reference to its Social Background*, PhD thesis, Cambridge, 1965

BRIGGS, J. & SELLERS, I.(eds), *Victorian Nonconformity*, Arnold, 1973

BROWNE, J., *History of Congregationalism in Norfolk & Suffolk*, Jarrold, 1877

COOPER, J.M., *The East Suffolk Railway*, Oakwood Press, 1982

DALE, R.W. (DALE E.W.W. ed), *History of English Congregationalism*, Hodder, 1907

DYMOND, D. & NORTHEAST, P., *A History of Suffolk*, Phillimore, 1985

EVANS, N., *The East Anglian Linen Industry*, Gower, 1985

FINER, S.E., *The Life and Times of Sir Edwin Chadwick*, London, 1952

FLINT, B., *Suffolk Windmills*, Boydell, 1979

GOOCH, M. & GOOCH, S., *The People of a Suffolk Town*, Halesworth, 1999

HALESWORTH TIMES, 1866-1878

JACOBS, L.C., *Constables of Suffolk, a brief history of policing in the county*, Suffolk Constabulary, 1992

JONES, R.T., *Congregationalism in England, 1662-1962*, Independent Press, 1962

LAWRENCE, R., *Southwold River*, Suffolk Books, 1990

LOCAL GOVERNMENT BOARD, *First Report* 1871 – Appendix: Paupers.

MEDICAL OFFICER OF THE PRIVY COUNCIL, *Fourth Report* 1861 – Vaccination in Suffolk

NEWBY, J.W., *History of Independency in Halesworth and District*, 1936

PARRY, K.L. (ed), *Companion to Congregational Praise*, London, 1953

SCARFE, N., *The Suffolk Landscape*, London, 1972

SPARKES, I., *Halesworth in the 19th Century*, 1999

SUFFOLK COUNTY COUNCIL, *Survey of Suffolk Parish History*, 1990

TAYLOR S.T., *The Diary of a Medical Student During the Victorian Period*, Norwich, 1927

THIRSK, J. & IMRAY, J., *Suffolk Farming in the 19th Century*, Suffolk Records Society, 1958

THOMPSON, D.M., *Nonconformity in the Nineteenth Century*, Routledge & Kegan Paul, London, 1972

TIMMINS, T.C.B. (ed), *Suffolk Returns, Census of Religious Worship 1851*, Suffolk Records Society, 1997

WATTS, M., *The Dissenters*, Volumes I & II, Oxford, 1978 and 1995

WEBB, S. & WEBB, B., *The Story of the King's Highway*, Longman, 1913

APPENDIX

Membership of Halesworth Independent Church 1866–1877

This list, compiled from the Numerical Register held at Halesworth United Reformed Church, Quay Street, gives details of all those who were members of the Church in Quay Street during the period covered by this book.

NAME	RESIDENCE	ADMITTED	LEFT	RETURNED	DIED	COMMENT
Adams, Eliza	Halesworth	1876	1885			To C of E
Adams, John	Halesworth	1864			1873	
Adams, Mary Ann	Halesworth	1874			1878	Mr Lay's servant
Aldred, William H	Halesworth	post-1852	1867 erased			
Aldrich, Mrs	Wissett	post-1854			1891	
Allen, Frederic	Halesworth	1877	1877			From NCC; excluded 1877
Allen, Mrs	Halesworth	1877	1880			From NCC
Andrews, Miss	Halesworth	1865	1871			To Cambridge
Archer, Fanny	Halesworth	1873	1875			To Ipswich
Archer, Mary Ann	Halesworth	1861	1867 erased			Mrs Alfred Taylor
Archer, Mrs Nelson	Halesworth	1873	1876			
Bailey, Miss Maria	Halesworth	1850	1873			Mrs Edward Sheldrake
Baker, George	Wissett	1868			1908	
Baker, Lucy	Halesworth	1869	1874			Mrs Brown; to Sheffield
Baker, Mrs G.	Wissett	1868			1902	
Baker, Mrs Samuel	Bungay Road	1872			1893	
Baldry, Mrs	Spexhall	1841	1874			

NCC–New Congregational Church B–Baptists C of E–Church of England PM–Primitive Methodists PR–Presbysterians W–Wesleyans

NAME	RESIDENCE	ADMITTED	LEFT	RETURNED	DIED	COMMENT
Baldry, Esther	Bramfield	1855	1871			Mrs Roper
Baldry, Robert Spence	Westhall	1866	1869			
Barber, Mrs Robert	Halesworth	1871			1874	
Bayles, Edgar	Grundisburgh	1870	1874			To Prince's Street, Norwich
Bedwell, John	Halesworth	1837	?	1864		To B. To Ipswich 1876
Bedwell, Mrs	Halesworth	1870	1876			To Ipswich
Bicker, Charles	Halesworth	1866	1867 erased			To Sudbury 1871
Bickus, Mary Ann	Henham	1863	1897 erased			To Southwold
Bird, Hannah	Wissett	1877	1880		1941	From NCC
Bird, William	Blythburgh	1819			1872	
Bishop, Deborah	Wissett	1868	1879			Mrs Clements, to Beccles
Bishop, Joseph	Wissett	1851			1886	
Bishop, Mrs Joseph	Wissett	1851			1881	
Blaxill, Mrs Fella	Halesworth	1866	1891			
Bloomfield, Mrs	Halesworth	1864	1867 erased		1875	To NCC
Boon, Edward	Holton	1871	1882			To Finsbury Circus
Boon, Emma	Holton	1868	1879			To W, Penge
Boon, Ernest	Holton	1875	1881			To London
Boon, Ezekiel	Holton	1875			1876	
Boon, Mrs Ezekial	Holton	1869	1884			To Victoria Park, London
Borrett, Mr Alfred, junior	Bramfield	1872			1907	

NCC–New Congregational Church B–Baptists C of E–Church of England PM–Primitive Methodists PR–Presbysterians W–Wesleyans

NAME	RESIDENCE	ADMITTED	LEFT	RETURNED	DIED	COMMENT
Boykett, Mary	Wissett	post-1852			1870	Mrs Kerrison
Brabbing, William	Blyford	1870	?			To B
Brown, John G.	Halesworth	1870	1875			To Crown Street, Ipswich
Brown, Mrs Elizabeth	Halesworth	1870			1920	
Brown, Mrs Samuel	Halesworth	1854			1904	
Brown, Samuel	Halesworth	1854			1884	Deacon & Treasurer, 1857
Brown, Susan	Chediston	1834			1879	
Brown, William S.	Halesworth	1872			1929	
Browne, Mary Louisa	Halesworth	1856	1874			To Yarmouth
Browne, Miss Elizabeth	Halesworth	1856/1890	1886			Mrs W.H. Ives, to Norwich
Browne, Miss Emily	Halesworth	1856	1868			To Holloway
Browne, Mrs R.	Halesworth	1856	1874			To Yarmouth
Butcher, Miss Charlotte	Upper Holton	1866	1871			Mrs Henry French
Butcher, Mrs Isaac	Upper Holton	1861			1871	
Butcher, Mrs Isaac	Wissett	1876			1879	
Byles, John	Halesworth	1877	1889	1898	1916	From NCC
Byles, Mrs	Halesworth	1877	1877	1879		From NCC
Cady, George	Chediston	1877	1890			
Carly, Betsy	Halesworth	1858	1871			
Chapman, A.J.	Halesworth	1877			1926	From NCC
Chapman, Mrs	Halesworth	1877			1925	From NCC

NCC–New Congregational Church   B–Baptists   C of E–Church of England   PM–Primitive Methodists   PR–Presbysterians   W–Wesleyans

NAME	RESIDENCE	ADMITTED	LEFT	RETURNED	DIED	COMMENT
Chapman, Sarah	Halesworth	post-1852			1872	Mrs Edward Harvey
Chason, Mary Ann	Halesworth	1866			1921	Mrs F. Haward, Wissett
Chipperfield, Elizabeth	Halesworth	1861	1882			To Manor Park, London
Chipperfield, Mrs N.	Halesworth	1861			1902	
Chipperfield, Nathan	Halesworth	1861			1902	Deacon 1896
Chipperfield, William	Halesworth	1836			1882	
Clapham, Mrs S.	Halesworth	post-1854				
Clapham, Mr Samuel	Halesworth	post-1854	1877			To Colchester
Clark, Mrs William	Westhall	1862			1877	
Clarke, John	Halesworth	1864			1896	
Clements, Charlotte	Holton	1835			1885	
Clements, John	Broadway	1861	1879			To Beccles
Cook, Caroline	Halesworth	1841	67/84 erased	1877		Mrs Harvey; to NCC
Cook, Mary Ann	Halesworth	1840	1867 erased	1877	1878	Mrs Rackham
Cornish, Henry	Halesworth	1857	1867 erased		1875	To NCC
Cornish, Miss Eliza	Halesworth	1873	1879			Mrs Phillips
Cornish, Mrs H.	Halesworth	1857	1867 erased			To NCC
Cowles, Martha	Halesworth	1868			1870	
Cowles, Mrs, junior	Halesworth	1877			1896	From NCC
Cowles, Sarah	Halesworth	1871			1873	
Crawford, Mrs Peter	Halesworth	1869	1885			To Ipswich, PR

NCC–New Congregational Church B–Baptists C of E–Church of England PM–Primitive Methodists PR–Presbysterians W–Wesleyans

NAME	RESIDENCE	ADMITTED	LEFT	RETURNED	DIED	COMMENT
Croft, Eliza	Halesworth	1877			1905	From NCC
Cullingford, Caroline	Halesworth	1852	1868 erased			Mrs J. Read
Cullingford, Mrs	Halesworth	1877			1921	From NCC
Cushion, Samuel	Wenhaston	1862			1880	
Danes, Maria	Halesworth	post-1852			1891	Mrs W. Thompson
Delf, Mrs	Sotherton	1852	1871			To Bungay
Eade, Mrs Samuel	Halesworth	1865	1867 erased	1871	1872	To NCC
Eade, Samuel	Halesworth	1865	1867 erased	1871	1904	To NCC
Edgeley, Amy	Halesworth	1875	1877			To PM
Edgley, Sarah	Halesworth	1864			1917	Mrs Clark (2)
Elworthy, Mrs George	Halesworth	1851			1877	
Elworthy, Harriett	Halesworth	1851			1882	
Etheridge, Harriett	Halesworth	1866	1867 erased			Mrs Kett, to PM
Etheridge, William	Chediston	post-1852	1868 erased			
Farrington, Miss Eliza	Halesworth	1873	1891			
Farrington, Mr Robert	Bramfield	1872	1869	1906	1914	
Farrington, Mrs Lydia	Halesworth	1863			1875	Mrs Robert Farrington
Farrow, Mrs Louisa	Broadway	1859			1874	
Fenn, Mr William	Westhall	1872			1886	
Fenn, Mrs James	Holton	1866			1894	
Fisher, Mr & Mrs Frdck	Halesworth	1871	1882			To C of E

NCC–New Congregational Church   B–Baptists   C of E–Church of England   PM–Primitive Methodists   PR–Presbyterians   W–Wesleyans

NAME	RESIDENCE	ADMITTED	LEFT	RETURNED	DIED	COMMENT
Foreman, Ellen	Halesworth	1874	1877			Mr Bedwell's servant
Foreman, Elvinah	Halesworth	post-1852	1867 erased			Mrs Day, NCC?
Francis, Elijah	Upper Holton	1861	1896			Deacon, 1884
Francis, Jemima	Upper Holton	1859	1900			Mrs J. Sparrow
Francis, Mrs Elijah	Halesworth	1871	1898			
Fuller, Mr Frederick	Bramfield	1872	1874			Left England
Gage, Mrs	Halesworth	1863	1868 erased			Reunited Framlingham Ch.
Gardner, Mr	Halesworth	1877			1882	From NCC
Gardner, Mrs	Halesworth	1877			1878	From NCC
Gayfer, Maria	Walpole	1863			1883	Mrs Wm Gayfer
Gayfer, William	Wenhaston	1838			1888	
George, William, junior	Cookley	1864	1876 erased			
Gibson, Mr & Mrs T.	Bramfield	1869	1871 erased			
Gooding, Miss Clara	Holton	1873	1875			Mrs Gooderham, Rumburgh
Goodwin, Miss	Halesworth	1866			1867	
Goodwin, Mrs John	Halesworth	1864			1874	
Gostling, John H.	Halesworth	1866	1867 erased	1877	1906	To NCC, Deacon 1884
Gostling, Mrs H.	Halesworth	1866	1867 erased	1877	1876	To NCC
Gregory, Emma	Halesworth	1877	1878			From NCC
Hadingham, Frederick	Halesworth	1877		1893		From NCC
Hadingham, Miss Annie	Saxmundham	1877	1882	*1882*	1950	From NCC

NCC–New Congregational Church B–Baptists C of E–Church of England PM–Primitive Methodists PR–Presbysterians W–Wesleyans

NAME	RESIDENCE	ADMITTED	LEFT	RETURNED	DIED	COMMENT
Hadingham, Mrs S.W.	Halesworth	1859	1867 erased	1877	1903	
Hadingham, Stephen W.	Halesworth	1858	1867 erased	1877	1909	Deacon 1897
Hall, Jane	Halesworth	1870	1897			Mrs Tovell?
Hart, Miss	Spexhall	1852	1882			Mrs Nurse
Hart, Mrs	Spexhall	1841/1861	1879			To Walpole. Mrs R. Haward
Harvey, Miss Selina	Halesworth	1877	1882			From NCC
Harvey, Caroline	Halesworth	1841	77/84 erased	1877		See Caroline Cook
Harvey, Joseph B.	Halesworth	1843	1867 erased	1877	1891	Deacon; to Stockwell 1884
Harvey, Miss Caroline	Halesworth	1877	1882			From NCC
Harvey, Miss Grace	Halesworth	1877	1884			To Stockwell
Harvey, Miss Sarah	Halesworth	1877	1889			To Stockwell
Haward, Mrs George	Bramfield	1850	1876			To Hastings
Haward, Arabella	Bramfield	1862	1874			Mrs Eley; to New Zealand
Haward, Caroline	Bramfield	1841	1871			Mrs Howes; to Norfolk
Haward, Caroline	Halesworth	1876	1877			To East Dulwich
Haward, Charles	Halesworth	1865	1867 erased	1877		From NCC
Haward, Charles	Bramfield	1834	1848	1876	1895	To B. NCC? Deacon 1877
Haward, Mrs Charles	Bramfield	1850			1874	
Haward, Emma	Halesworth	1864	1868			To Lowestoft
Haward, Francis Edwin	Bramfield	1865	1867 & 1877	1875		To Farnham; to Hereford
Haward, Frederick	Wissett	1874			1930	

NCC–New Congregational Church B–Baptists C of E–Church of England PM–Primitive Methodists PR–Presbysterians W–Wesleyans

NAME	RESIDENCE	ADMITTED	LEFT	RETURNED	DIED	COMMENT
Haward, George	Bramfield	1840	1876			To Hastings. Deacon 1850
Haward, Hannah Sophia	Bramfield	1870	1876			To Hastings
Haward, Jane	Bramfield	1866	1876			To Hastings
Haward, Jemima	Halesworth	1862	1871			
Haward, Louisa	Halesworth	1838			1867	Wife of S. Haward, tailor
Haward, Louisa	Bramfield	1840	1877/1891	1881		Sister of George Haward
Haward, Maria Louisa	Bramfield	1874	1896			To Aberdeen
Haward, Mrs Charles	Bramfield	1850			1874	
Haward, Mrs Samuel	Wissett	1869			1884	
Haward, Rebbecca	Mells Hill	1865	1874			Mrs Tho Sale, to Lowestoft
Haward, Robert Ebenezer	Mells Hill	1870			1936	Secretary 1876-1923
Haward, Susan	Halesworth	1866	1871 erased			
Haward, Susannah	Mells Hill	1862	1876			Mrs E. Bayles; to Norwich
Haward, Walter	Wissett	1873	1882	1887	1926	To Canada
Haward, William	Bramfield	1869			1877	
Hill, Mrs	Halesworth	1877			1884	From NCC
Hollingsworth, John	Halesworth	1869	1873			To Bedford
Hollingsworth, Mrs	Halesworth	1871	1873			To Bedford
Hopkinson, Miss	Halesworth	1877	1882			From NCC
Hunt, Mrs	Spexhall	1852	1887			To C of E
Hurren, Harriett	Halesworth	1841	1871			To London

NCC–New Congregational Church B–Baptists C of E–Church of England PM–Primitive Methodists PR–Presbysterians W–Wesleyans

NAME	RESIDENCE	ADMITTED	LEFT	RETURNED	DIED	COMMENT
Hurren, Sarah	Halesworth	1840	1868 excluded	1877	1880	From NCC?
Ives, Walter Henry	Halesworth	1861	1886	1890	1912	Deacon 1896
Jackson, James	Wissett	post-1852			1892	
Jackson, Miss Emily	Halesworth	1877	1878			From NCC; W
Jackson, Mrs James	Wissett	post-1852			1892	
Johnson, William	Halesworth	1873			1880	
Kent, Mary Ann	Halesworth	1861	1889			Mrs W. Bishop; to Canada
Kent, Mrs Thomas	Halesworth	post-1854			1898	
Last, Miss E.	Halesworth	post-1852	1867 erased		1879	Mrs Mannell
Lay, James	Wenhaston	1861			1888	
Lay, Mrs James	Wenhaston	1861			1883	
Lefsey, Catherine	Halesworth	1837			1889	Mrs W. George
Lincolne, Napier	Halesworth	1840	1871			To Ely
Lines, Marianne	Upper Holton	1870	1871 erased			
Lines, Mary Ann	Broadway	1861	?			To Stoke Newington
Lock, Mrs Samuel	Bramfield	1868			1905	From W
Long, Mr	Halesworth	1855	1867 erased		1869	To NCC
Long, Mrs	Halesworth	1855	1867 erased		1878	To NCC
Lovell, Elizabeth	Halesworth	1877	1892			To C of E
Lunnis, Mr James	Halesworth	1864	1867 erased			To NCC
Mayhew, Robert	Wissett	1869	1880			

NCC–New Congregational Church B–Baptists C of E–Church of England PM–Primitive Methodists PR–Presbysterians W–Wesleyans

NAME	RESIDENCE	ADMITTED	LEFT	RETURNED	DIED	COMMENT
Mills, Henrietta Caroline	Halesworth	1857	1879			To Stowmarket
Mills, Sophia	Chediston	post-1852				Mrs Etheridge
Moore, Francis	Halesworth	1867	1870			To Norwich
Moore, Mrs F.	Halesworth	1867	1870			To Norwich
Moss, Samuel	Halesworth	1865	1878			To Bungay
Nurse, James	St Andrew	1857	1882			To Sutton, Surrey
Page, Celia	Wenhaston	1863			1874	Mrs Charles Eves
Page, Charlotte	Halesworth	1868			1868	
Page, Elizabeth	Spexhall	1856			1877	Mrs William Reid
Page, Emma	Halesworth	1857	1871			
Page, Mary	Linstead	post-1833			1869	
Page, William	Spexhall	1851			1884	
Pashley, Ellen Maria	Walpole	post-1852	1867 erased			Mrs W.H. Aldred
Peck, Miss	Bramfield	1877	1878			From NCC; to Lowestoft
Pepper, Elizabeth	Halesworth	1862	1871 & 1884	1875		To B Tunstall
Prime, Mrs E.	Halesworth	post-1852	1867 erased	1877	1877	To NCC
Puttock, George	Bramfield	1871	1889			
Rackham, Charles	Halesworth	1864	1871 erased			
Rackham, Mrs, senior	Halesworth	1857	1867 erased		1875	To NCC
Read, James	Halesworth	1877			1910	From NCC
Reeve, Sarah	Upper Holton	1862			1875	Mrs Thomas Reeve

NCC–New Congregational Church B–Baptists C of E–Church of England PM–Primitive Methodists PR–Presbyterians W–Wesleyans

NAME	RESIDENCE	ADMITTED	LEFT	RETURNED	DIED	COMMENT
Reeve, Thomas	Spexhall	1863	1878			To Canterbury
Rignall, Mrs W.	Halesworth	1869			1908	
Rignall, William	Halesworth	1869			1895	
Rockhill, Martha	Holton	1838			1890	Member 52 years
Roe, Benjamin	Halesworth	1859	1862	1877	1903	From NCC; Deacon 1877
Roe, Mrs	Halesworth	1877			1908	From NCC
Sago, Celia	Wenhaston	1863			1874	Mrs Charles Eves
Sago, Mr J., junior	Broadway	1873				Deacon 1910
Sago, Mrs	Upper Holton	1871			1893	
Sago, Mrs J., junior	Broadway	1873			1917	
Sago, William	Spexhall	1851			1884	
Sago, Mrs William	Bungay Road	1872			1887	
Sale, Thomas	Halesworth	1867	1874		1889	To Lowestoft
Sallows, William	Westhall	1865	1879			
Scraggs, Kerenhappuck	Halesworth	1863			1885	Mrs David Scraggs
Self, John	Holton	1870	1872			To Islington
Self, Elizabeth Ann	Halesworth	1873	1874			To London
Sewell, Mary Ann	Spexhall	1840/1858	1867 erased			NCC?
Shade, Mary Ann	Wissett	1864	1871			To London
Shade, Mrs Charles	Blyford	1872	1878			
Shade, Louisa	Halesworth	post-1854	1884			To Beccles

NCC–New Congregational Church B–Baptists C of E–Church of England PM–Primitive Methodists PR–Presbysterians W–Wesleyans

NAME	RESIDENCE	ADMITTED	LEFT	RETURNED	DIED	COMMENT
Shade, Nathaniel	Halesworth	post-1854	1884			To Beccles
Silverton, John	Halesworth	1864			1872	
Silverton, Mrs	Halesworth	1864			1889	
Skinner, Mr George	Walpole	1872	erased?			
Skinner, Mrs George	Walpole	1872	erased?			
Smith, Hammett	Wissett	1871			1890	
Smith, Samuel	Halesworth	1858	1867 erased	1877	1916	To NCC
Smith, Samuel	Halesworth	1864	1867 erased		1873	
Spurr, Thomas	Halesworth	1876	1877			To Debenham
Stannard, Hannah	Spexhall	1862			1894	Mrs David Stannard
Stannard, David, junior	Spexhall	1876	1880			To Lowestoft
Starke, Mrs	Halesworth	1877			1877	From NCC
Stopher, Mary	Halesworth	1841			1882	Mrs William Stopher
Taylor, Ann	Wissett	1876	1879			Mrs Jordan
Taylor, Mrs D.	Halesworth	post-1852	1875			To Leiston
Taylor, Mrs William	Wissett	1873			1900	
Thurlow, Mrs M.	Walpole	post-1852			1885	
Took, Mrs R.	Halesworth	post-1854	1868 erased		1876	
Upton, Charlotte	Halesworth	1856			1882	Mrs Wlliam Upton
Vesey, Richard	Halesworth	1869	1871			To Lowestoft
Wall, Mr J.H.	Halesworth	1876	1878			To Fakenham

NCC–New Congregational Church B–Baptists C of E–Church of England PM–Primitive Methodists PR–Presbysterians W–Wesleyans

NAME	RESIDENCE	ADMITTED	LEFT	RETURNED	DIED	COMMENT
Waller, Josiah	Halesworth	1860	1867 erased			To NCC
Waller, Mrs Josiah	Halesworth	1860	1867 erased			To NCC
Westgate, Miss	Halesworth	1877	1905			From NCC
White, Robert	Halesworth	1866	1870			To Braintree
Wigg, Mrs W.	Halesworth	post-1852	1868 erased	1871		To NCC?
Wigg, William	Halesworth	1866			1890	
Wight, Mrs Susan	Halesworth	post-1854			1870	
Wild, Mrs Thomas	Halesworth	1852	1875			To Tacket Street, Ipswich
Williams, Mrs	Halesworth	1851	?	1872	1884	To B
Wood, Mrs D.	Wissett	post-1854			1877	
Woodgate, Mrs	Halesworth	1877			1899	From NCC
Woolnough, Miss Anna	Halesworth	1873			1875	

NCC–New Congregational Church   B–Baptists   C of E–Church of England   PM–Primitive Methodists   PR–Presbysterians   W–Wesleyans